INSIDE THE
INDIAN BUSINESS MIND

INSIDE THE INDIAN BUSINESS MIND

A TACTICAL GUIDE FOR MANAGERS

KATHERINE C. ZUBKO
RAJ R. SAHAY

JAICO PUBLISHING HOUSE
Ahmedabad Bangalore Bhopal Chennai
Delhi Hyderabad Kolkata Lucknow Mumbai

Published by Jaico Publishing House
A-2 Jash Chambers, 7-A Sir Phirozshah Mehta Road
Fort, Mumbai - 400 001
jaicopub@jaicobooks.com
www.jaicobooks.com

© Katherine C. Zubko and Raj R. Sahay

Originally published in hard cover by Praeger,
an imprint of ABC-CLIO, LLC
Santa Barbara, CA

Published in arrangement with
ABC-CLIO, LLC, Santa Barbara, CA
All rights reserved

INSIDE THE INDIAN BUSINESS MIND
ISBN 978-81-7992-964-3

First Jaico Impression: 2011

No part of this book may be reproduced or transmitted in
any form or by any means electronic or mechanical
including photocopying, reprinting or on any information
storage and retrieval system, without permission in writing from
Jaico Publishing House and ABC-CLIO, LLC.

Printed by
Kaveri Print Process Pvt. Ltd.
114, Patparganj Industrial Area, Delhi-92

To our parents

Contents

Illustrations	ix
Preface	xi
Acknowledgments	xvii
Introduction: Entering the Market	xxi
1 In the Land of Curry: An Age-Old Cuisine	1
2 A Recipe for Business Success: The Most Important Ingredients	19
3 Ingredient 1: Hospitality	25
4 Ingredient 2: Role Expectations	35
5 Ingredient 3: Business Caste or Hierarchy	45
6 Ingredient 4: Project Process and Management	55
7 Ingredient 5: Leadership and Teamwork	65
8 Ingredient 6: Risk and Action	75
9 Ingredient 7: The Pursuit of Wealth	85
10 Ingredient 8: The Original Business Contract	97
11 Ingredient 9: Nonconfrontational Negotiation	109
12 Ingredient 10: Cultural Views of Time and Space	119
13 Ingredient 11: Women in the Workplace	131
14 Seasoned to Perfection, or How to Mix Your Ingredients with Success	143

Conclusion	153
Appendix: Facts About India: Menu Options	157
Notes	167
Bibliography	175
Index	177

Illustrations

1. Map of India, 2.
2. Flower garlands, sold for *pujas*, marriages, and formal greetings for VIPs, 26.
3. Food and drink as forms of hospitality: a *thali* meal plate from South India and tea being served in an office meeting, 29.
4. Pilgrims climbing the steps up to the temple of the Hindu god Murugan in the South Indian town of Palani, having recently passed the rest stop pavilion, 56.
5. Indian businesspeople working together as a team, 66.
6. Lakshmi, Hindu goddess of wealth, with rupees at her feet, 86.
7. Talisman of profit: (left) the display of Hindu gods, goddesses, and a garlanded portrait of a holy man behind the cash receipts booth at a restaurant in India, and (right) the display of the "first dollar bill" of profit and good luck bills on the wall behind the cash register in an American ice cream shop, 87.
8. Businesses as the domain of the gods: (top) shops in India named after the Hindu gods Laxmi (Lakshmi) and Krishna, and (bottom) poster prints of the Hindu gods appearing behind the cash counter at a clothing shop, 88.
9. Fire sacrifice being conducted by local priests at a Hindu temple in Greensboro, North Carolina, in 2009, 98.
10. *Puja* in the workplace: worship being conducted near computers at the beginning of the stock market year in Mumbai, India, 125.

Preface

Every book has a starting point. For the one that you are holding in your hands right now that point of conception was in the foreign language section of the Boston Public Library in Copley Square. One crisp fall day in 2005, two people had followed the arrows matching the appropriate call number to meet in an aisle of tall metal bookshelves lined with dictionaries and grammars from Arabic to Swahili. Up on a ladder, Raj was pulling out the title *Teach Yourself Hindi* just as Kate rounded the corner of the aisle.

When the pair realized they had been seeking the same book, a conversation began. Raj was in the process of helping a client who would be traveling to India on business. The client's company had expectations about what the tasks and outcomes should be, but had not provided much training on how to achieve those goals within a completely different cultural setting. While Raj was giving one-on-one advice on how to negotiate cultural issues, he also was in search of resources to help his client acquire some language skills before her departure.

Kate was a Ph.D. student in the process of writing her dissertation on South Asian religion and culture. After returning from conducting research in Chennai, she would often get calls from the partners or friends of colleagues who were working in the private sector or for nonprofit organizations. These people were being sent to India as part of their work, but they felt that their places of employment were not preparing them for the cultural issues they could encounter in trying to meet the goals of their business interactions. In the midst of the daily writing routine, she began to meet people for coffee or talk by phone to answer questions and give advice. This had led her to the library that day to assess new sources she could offer to these people.

The amount of misperceptions about India and stereotypes that both of us witnessed in our work and travel experiences was a major topic of our conversations. One day we began to list several of these, many of which had come from some of our personal narratives as an Indian man working in the United States and abroad, and as an American woman working in India, as well as hearing the stories of our colleagues and friends.

Raj's Story

Arriving in the United States in the early 1990s to enter an MBA program, I encountered my share of cultural shock on campus as well as in corporate settings that left me shocked, surprised, and on some occasions totally bewildered.

Coming from a social background that was very hierarchical and a culture that inculcated a great deal of respect for elders and teachers, I was astonished to see students addressing their professors by their first names. Once I went to see a finance professor, Charles Finnerty, who suggested that I should call him Chuck when I addressed him as "sir," which probably made him uncomfortable. On another occasion I felt aghast when my classmates refused an accounting professor's request to cancel a class to attend a personal emergency since they were not interested in a makeup class over the weekend. I was at my wit's end to see my classmates consuming food and drinks during lectures and sometimes sitting with their legs raised up on chairs, pointing their feet in the direction of the teacher.

Later at work, although I admired the straightforward talk and love for punctuality of my colleagues, I was intrigued by their approach to relationships, personal as well as professional. To me, it seemed transactional and had a rather short-term orientation. I interpreted love for fierce individuality and total freedom as a bit immoral since it ignored family and larger social values. At the same time, when I went back to work in India for a few years, I confronted some of the deeply ingrained local cultural habits at work that should not have affected me but they did. They made me uneasy and a misfit amidst my own people, such as a casual attitude toward timeliness and hierarchical work environments bordering on reverence for the boss to name a few. I could very well visualize the plight of American or European managers working with their counterparts and teams in India.

My experiences and cultural encounters in corporate environments both in the United States and India had often provoked me to imagine a situation and the outcome when the two cultures would collide. I could clearly see the confrontation and confusion ruling the roost unless there is an honest and concerted effort *sans* prejudice to understand one another as people and human beings. I was both a student and a victim of the chasm separating the two sides but the idea to embark on a journey to bridge this gap, though germinating in my head for quite a while, didn't reach its fruition until I ran into Kate that afternoon in 2005 at the Boston Public Library.

Kate's Story

I landed in the middle of the night in India for the first time during the academic year that would witness the turning of the millennium. In fall 1999, I had earned a one-year travel grant to expand upon the two years of graduate studies in South Asian religion and culture I had just completed at Harvard University. On this first trip, as well as another subsequent 10-month trip for research for my Ph.D., I encountered several issues regarding logistics that my academic studies had no way of preparing me to handle.

The first few months of research involved setting up interviews with several local people involved in the support of arts and culture—not just performers, but also program organizers, grant agencies, auditorium board members, arts magazine editors, and corporate and individual donors. Without a liaison, I attempted to call different institutional bodies to clarify information and arrange meetings. Inevitably, I would be passed along until I reached a person who would agree to meet with me to answer my questions.

I would show up at the designated time, with my digital recorder and notebook, and I would be asked to have a seat. It did not matter if I was in someone's home or at an office, often tea was brought while I waited. Many times the person whom I had an appointment with was not available at all or not even present and I was asked to come back another time. "When?" I would ask, with the reply being some vague time frame—this afternoon, tomorrow morning, and so on. An exact time was not usually given.

In the beginning, I had tried to line up several appointments on a single day, which did not work very well. If people showed up late, I had to decide whether to cut short the interview to go on to the next meeting, or call and reschedule. If I went to the next meeting on time, often that person would not be available. When I did meet with people, within 10 minutes I found out that this was not the person who had the information I needed, and asked to speak to someone who could answer my questions. "Oh, yes" or "we'll see" were common responses, even when sometimes the answer was really a "no."

These early experiences were frustrating, and I resisted drawing negative conclusions that would not have resolved the roadblocks I was facing. My American cultural background brought expectations about time and appointments, access to information, and even types of direct communication. I could choose to hold tight to these expectations, or even feed into stereotypes of punctuality and what might be perceived as dishonest—if something can't be done, a "no" would be the more direct or "honest" answer. I could remain frustrated, or reevaluate these expectations and see if there were clues I was missing that would help me complete my work. If I could understand why and then learn how to negotiate within the system, I would be able to create more successful interactions.

Moving Past Stereotypes

Our monthly conversations led to the realization that the types of resources available on the market for people going to India on business were not sufficient to help people navigate past the stereotypes. We had scanned the shelves and bestseller lists, finding many books describing the overall big picture in the interlinked globalized economies of the world—India and China were both in the spotlight as economists, journalists, and political theorists marked seismic shifts and trends, and digested them to the general readership market. As we continued our hunt and scoured the Internet, many etiquette books and articles were also available—lists of do's and don'ts that people should memorize. Some books on international negotiation also provided, in bullet point format, some tips on communication styles and gestures that should be engaged or avoided in different countries. Third, there were also books available on "Doing Business in India"—a promising title or subtitle that caught our attention. Each of these genres is helpful on a certain level, but we found that many of them hardly discussed culture beyond the stereotypes or to the degree of depth necessary to really prepare people.

While the United States dominates the attention of Indian executives through business school case studies, cable TV, media channels, magazines, and the Internet, giving them a broad familiarity with the popular culture, U.S. executives and Americans at large are quite uninformed about India, its history, and culture. They know about India and Indians primarily through Hollywood movies, their local Indian food restaurant, the consumer explosion of Indian goods in style and design magazines and clothing, and to some extent on the basis of limited interactions with the immigrant Indian American community. Most Americans know India for the beautiful Taj Mahal. Religious seekers are drawn by the promise of its spiritual centers in Varanasi, Haridwar, Rishikesh, and the Himalayas, and some even write up their experiences that become *New York Times* bestsellers. But for most Americans, India is still the land of snake charmers, spiritual gurus, yoga, holy cows, and karma.

Raj and I knew firsthand that the lack of solid cultural information about India, along with stereotypes and misperceptions, creates major roadblocks in the interactions of businesspeople between our two cultures. We could fill a whole book demonstrating the problems these misperceptions cause just in the business environment alone. We realized that in order to recognize and move past these obstacles, it would be more effective to start by highlighting some of the outstanding features of Indian culture. We would then translate these cultural features in such a way as to not only break past those stereotypes, but provide templates that avoid the problems and misperceptions to begin with and identifies and corrects those already in place.

While adequate cultural information does prevent problems, and can be used to troubleshoot and resolve many snags, having a high level of cultural awareness is only a starting point. Any cross-cultural endeavor is bound to run into some unexpected issues. Even the writing of this book as authors from different cultures led to differences that we had no way of knowing about until we started collaborating on a project together. For example, once we had our cultural templates chosen, we were brainstorming different case examples that would best illustrate the translation of these ideas into business contexts. We found out we had very different approaches: Raj often chose to highlight tried and true case studies from large corporate models, and touched upon general public knowledge drawn from movies, news items, and history he absorbed without reference to specific sources. Kate, on the other hand, sought cases based on individual experiences that, with a personal voice, either Raj or his colleagues had experienced or could provide the seed for a narrative. In both of these approaches, the aim was to reach our main audience—the American manager traveling to India on business. Which approach would work best? How would each of these approaches serve to translate the models into practical tools?

In this process, we discovered that each of our approaches was based on a culture-specific preference for different types of knowledge to serve as the highest form of authority. In American culture, individual experience is valued for its insight and unique perspective. In Indian culture, the highest compliment is absorption and acknowledgement of those who have gone before as having more value than one's own narrative.

Neither of these approaches is wrong. They just place the emphasis in different places in terms of cultural ideas of what holds more weight. We were frustrated at first, in that we felt each of us were unable to communicate well. Once we discovered it was a difference in cultural approaches, we were able to begin the process of mixing the two styles to come up with what we hope are not only the best illustrations of each cultural template, but an accurate representation of different cultural approaches. You will see a bit of both here, from Raj's ahistorical overview of the culture of India in chapter one, to Kate's structural features that include for each ingredient a bullet point summary and inclusion of very specific individual voices. Cultural translation requires a willingness to collaborate from both sides to be able to find common ground.

Overall, the cultural models suggested in this book are the best tools we have to offer in order for you to gain an important versatility with which to adapt to any business situation within which you find yourself. This book identifies and translates tools that are valued and recognizable within Indian culture as strategies that will improve your interactions and transactions with your Indian business associates. Happy and successful travels!

Acknowledgments

This volume has benefited from a network of professional and personal support, as well as the voluntary generosity of several informants who work between the cultures of India and the United States. We are grateful to those who have engaged us in discussions and comments that have shaped both the substance and presentation of the ideas found on these pages for the better. In particular, we wish to thank Jeff Olson, who took a leap by believing in our proposal; Brian Romer, who generously granted time for the project to reach fruition; Erin Ryan, and all those involved at Praeger-Greenwood Press (now under ABC-CLIO) involved in the production process of the manuscript. In addition, each of us in turn wishes to thank the following.

Raj: I owe deep gratitude to a number of friends, colleagues, and well-wishers who have encouraged and supported me. The following are preeminent and deserve my heartfelt thanks and recognition in particular.

My dear friend and former colleague at Bank of India, Dinbandhu (Andrews) Mohapatra, who foresaw my vision for the book and believed that I had the intellectual abilities and background to take it up.

Pradipta Borgohain, a doctoral student in English literature who became a close friend during my MBA days at the University of Illinois at Urbana-Champaign, and was my bouncing board for almost daily discussions on Indo-U.S. cultural differences and adaptation challenges faced by international students like me. He encouraged me to delve deep into the issue of culture and examine its interconnectedness with the world of business.

Alecca and Gabriela for being such good Samaritans; they spared time from their busy schedules and provided great insights into the challenges female entrepreneurs and workers may face in India.

Venkat Iyer for always responding to my India-related business questions, not to mention sharing his views on the workings of business hierarchy in India.

Dimple Gupta for her affection and support, who always egged me on to keep challenging myself with her animated discussions on the subject matter.

Katherine Zubko (Kate), my friend and business partner, without her this project may always have remained a nonstarter and none of this would be possible.

Also: Patty Grogan, Vibha Desai, Hemant Sarangi, Alok Bharadwaj, Ajay Asthana, Raj Bhatia, Ashok Deshpande, Vrajlal Sapovadia, Sujoya Basu, Anna Botelho, Jasmine Bharathan, Lalita de Goederen, Noreen Van Holstein, Marianne Noa Akkerman, Milena Mlakar, Patricia Chandrashekar. Thanks a lot for your kind wishes and words of encouragement.

Kate: I am grateful to many teachers, colleagues, friends, and family who have contributed in both large and small ways to this work. Forgive me for not naming everyone individually, as the list has grown too numerous.

While some of the ideas for this book were hatched in business meetings with Raj, the original book proposal would not have been written if it were not for the support of the Anderson-Alboim family, who encouraged me to go ahead and send this out even while finishing my dissertation under their generous care and company.

Thanks also to many readers who have provided useful feedback and constructive sounding boards for the development of ideas, including Malini, Pankaj, Hemant, Kirti, Laura, Prema, Katrina, and MP Kate. Special thanks to Preetha for her networking skills and willingness to introduce helpful contacts; Joyce, a great mentor and friend, who also provided a timely assortment of reviewers; Sushmitha and the Kanukurthi family for answering random inquiries and providing excellent hospitality; Courtney Gauthier for her timely assistance with bibliographic details; Yunus Wesley, who worked diligently on the index; Stacy Blake-Beard, who trusted me with her current ongoing work on mentoring; and Raj for his hard work and partnership in this project. Also, this book would be nowhere near as polished without the rapid turnaround of the manuscript, marked with the honest, insightful, and constructive comments of Yamini Atmavilas.

Colleagues from my one-year visiting professor position at University of North Carolina–Greensboro and my new home as an assistant professor at UNC–Asheville have provided invaluable advice about contracts, time to write, and encouragement to complete the project while fulfilling academic responsibilities of teaching and service.

In addition, I am grateful for the kind words and deeds of Heather, Laura, Shannon, Sucharita, Kristen, and Shelly. Special thanks to my creative sister, Natalia, for her graphic design skills and unconditional support in all endeavors, and to the rest of my family—Lodewyk, Pamela, Zack, Berangere, Sophia, and Grant—for always believing in me.

Introduction: Entering the Market

Your bags are packed and you have a boarding ticket in hand. A few months earlier, you received word that you would be going to India on business, maybe for your first time or your fifth. Visas have been arranged. Language lessons may have moved to the top of your MP3's playlist. In addition to putting together any presentations and plans, a running list of do's and don'ts runs through your head haphazardly, beginning to jumble together. Besides wondering if the project will go smoothly, and thinking through any areas to troubleshoot, you also may be concerned about the food and water, the heat, and whether you will by mistake cross some unknown cultural taboo and offend your Indian colleagues. Friends and coworkers offer advice, both solicited and unsolicited. The company may have handed you a manual on things to know about life in India, or bought you a few books. As you sit there in the airport, you may be asking yourself: What do I really need to know to be able to adapt to any business situation in India? Do I have the tools I need for a successful trip?

The two most overlooked strategic tools that foreign managers often forget to pack are inseparable: **culture** and **context.** Accurate and practical facts about the culture within which you will be working are essential. And yet this key information can become trivial unless you know when, where, and how to use your knowledge of culture within and across appropriate contexts. If you do not include these two indivisible tools in your toolbox, getting things done efficiently and successfully is statistically harder to do and more costly.

Let's explore a few of the complexities of the relationship between these two tools further, as it is not so simple. For example, what is **culture?** The category of culture is so broad that it includes history, religion, arts, literature and language, dress, food, and customs found in different regions of India, among other features. The diversity and breadth of Indian culture would be a daunting task to understand even a portion of in the weeks leading up to your trip. It could take a lifetime to gain a high level of expertise in Indian culture. How then do you identify the most useful aspects of culture? How much do you need to understand about these cultural features in order to successfully navigate business in India?

With time in mind, you may have turned to etiquette books that give you in bullet point format some of the cultural information, as well as a list of do's and don'ts—maybe with or without explanations. For example, a list might include such statements as:

> Do bring a gift.
> Don't expect people to be punctual to meetings.
> Don't expect to hear "no" when someone disagrees with you.
> Do find the highest person in the pecking order with which to negotiate.

This may seem like great information, and sometimes it is accurate, but not always. There are several pieces missing when you try and memorize a list of rules. In many cases, this list only raises more unanswered questions: When do I bring a gift? What should that gift be? How do I interpret if someone disagrees with me? How do I negotiate the hierarchy? How do I locate the top person, and is that person really the best person to be talking with to get things done? And then, there is the question, will I remember this list of rules in the middle of a meeting when the pressure is building?

While helpful advice can be found in these time-saving lists, the crucial missing piece is our second tool, **context.** You need enough information to be able to interpret any situation within which you find yourself before knowing how to adapt in order to improve the success of that interaction at that moment. Etiquette lists simply do not give you that foundation, and may end up misleading you or creating more problems, rather than saving time and resources. Applying cultural information in the right contexts requires sharpening your awareness, patience, and keeping a sense of humor as you begin to adapt your insights across new situations within which you find yourself.

This book offers a different approach that we believe will exponentially increase your potential for creating strong, successful business partnerships. Whether working with investors, teams of colleagues, or supervising outsourced staff, the cultural models presented in this book take into account the different contexts of business interactions.

This book contains 11 cultural norms we have identified as primary to understanding Indian culture. While there are many more to choose from within the diversity of the culture, we chose these features for their prevalence in affecting the mindsets and behavior of many of your South Asian colleagues and teams. Our aim is to not only explain these ideas, but to translate them directly into tools that can be utilized to help you and your commercial ventures succeed in the Indian context.

When people think "India," they often think of some experience with Indian cuisine—spicy, sweet, and savory offerings at a town's local restaurant. Due to this natural association, we chose to call these 11 cultural norms "ingredients." Each ingredient exists as a separate idea with its own history and distinct attributes. In practice, these ingredients are mixed together in unique ways depending on the context. Once you know the properties of the different ingredients, you will be able to add or subtract them to create just the right taste to be able to interpret and negotiate well in each situation. You will be able to determine how each factor may be at work, as well as learn how to mix the ingredients yourself like a master chef to produce the desired outcome.

Many of these ingredients are descriptive of foundational ideas that are pervasive in the culture. Because of the prominence of Hinduism, many of the features discussed are connected to this religious worldview. In certain cases, there is also a prescriptive element—some cultural ingredients exist as an ideal with a range of applications. By utilizing some of these ingredients, you may gain new approaches to leadership, be able to support the process of a project, or apply ideas toward risk assessment or negotiations that create successful, recognizable strategies that are respected in many Indian contexts.

Not all the cultural ingredients here are applicable in all situations. With practice, you will be able to know which ones, as templates, are at work or which ones to use yourself. These cultural models provide the tools to adapt to any situation. A little knowledge can go a long way to impress your South Asian colleagues—even greeting people with "Namaste" or attempting to eat with your fingers in some contexts produces instant cultural capital.

Chapter one provides a brief overview of the breadth of Indian culture, while chapter two gives a summary of each of the 11 particular cultural ingredients we have chosen to highlight. We address any general patterns regarding these ingredients, as well as information about why we chose these 11, out of the hundreds of choices possible. Each ingredient is then expanded upon in turn in its own chapter that explains the concept, its background, and context, as well as demonstrates its influence in various business cases we have constructed. Some of these examples are based on real life business models gathered from documented sources, while others are based on the seed of an experience that one of us participated in or encountered in the experiences of our colleagues. This book is filled with real life stories of those who have been on the ground in India learning to identify and negotiate many of the cultural features discussed in these chapters.

After all the ingredients have been introduced, chapter 14 draws attention to situations in which several of these cultural ingredients are identifiably at work and influencing the situation. After some concluding thoughts, we have also added an appendix that points to some of the many other cultural ingredients that may need to be explored when working in particular regions or industries within the country.

Overall, we hope this book provides you access to the missing ingredients you need to create and sustain successful business ventures with your Indian business partners. No matter where you are at in the process—just thinking about new markets in India, meeting your colleagues for the first time in person in their work environment rather than by phone and video, or have already been steadily building relationships for a few years with several branches, factories, and headquarters in place, this book provides tools for all stages of business.

Chapter 1

In the Land of Curry: An Age-Old Cuisine

India is one of the oldest civilizations of the world, emerging out of the Indus Valley Civilization that dates to 2500–1500 B.C.E.[1] The tumultuous tale of the Indian subcontinent spans nearly 4,000 years of recorded history, which is full of vicissitudes, conquests and defeats, achievements and downfalls. A rich mosaic of human endeavors, the country stands as a testament to the supremacy of the human spirit. It's a theater where history and geography have collided in constant convulsions, dynasties and empires changed quick hands and fates, and the destinies of people were erased and rewritten with blood and sweat many times over. India is a microcosm, a civilization unto itself, quite daunting and challenging but very welcoming in its overall character.

Lately, Indian culture is becoming one of the most recognizable imports to the United States (well before the *Slumdog Millionaire* effect). People know it when they see it, but what is "Indian culture"? There are many typical aspects that contribute to culture as a way of life, including: food, dress, language, religion, and the arts. In India, as elsewhere, these cultural features take on a diversity of expressions within different regions of the country. These regional expressions have acquired unique characteristics that over time manifested through an amalgam of local cultures based on occupation, caste, religion, and the size of various communities. These local cultures merge into larger regional identities and eventually into the diversity of India's composite national culture, a rich tapestry embellished by many varied and beautiful subcultures consisting of thousands of religious rituals, social norms, timeless traditions, colorful customs, and lyrical dialects.

A Date with History

In order to understand the multitude of cultural influences, it is a good idea to start with a brief mention of some key historical aspects. This is

2 Inside the Indian Business Mind

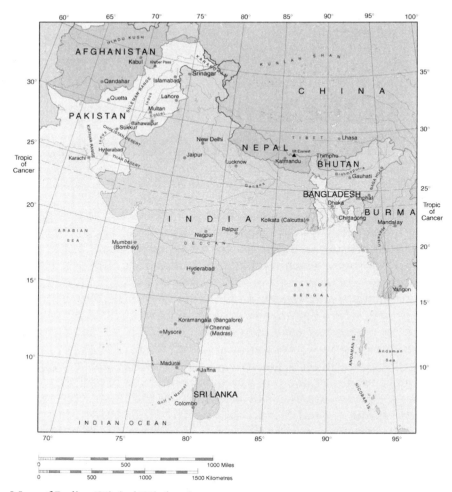

Map of India. (Digital Wisdom)

not meant to be a comprehensive outline, but demonstrates the variety of ruling powers and populations that factor into a broader cultural understanding.

While the history of the Indian subcontinent can be traced back to the advanced urban civilization of the Indus Valley, in its long history, India has also gone through cycles of conquests and migrations. The Vedic period saw an influx of nomadic Indo-Aryans from the Caucasus region, bringing with them the language of Sanskrit, horses, and the hierarchy of the caste system. Muslim military leaders, starting with Mahmud of Ghur of the Slave dynasty and followed by Khilji,

Tughlaq, and Lodhi dynasties ruled parts of India until 1526 C.E. when Babur established the Mughal Empire after defeating Ibrahim Lodi. Many parts of India functioned as small coexisting feudal states governed by local Hindu or Muslim rulers, which at times would form alliances or be consolidated under a centralized authority, only to break apart again. The fluxes of power are much like you would find anywhere in the world.

The two modern-day empires preceding independent nationhood were headed by the Mughals and the British. The Mughal emperors ruled India until the Europeans arrived on the scene, driven by their interests in trade at first. India became a prized trophy over which the Portuguese, French, Dutch, and English fought fiercely, but in the end the British came out victorious. The British crushed the 1857 Indian Revolt supported by the last Mughal emperor, Bahadur Shah Zafar, and exiled him to Burma (present-day Myanmar) where he later died. The British ruled over India until its independence in August 1947 when the subcontinent was partitioned into a majority Hindu India and a majority Muslim Pakistan. Later, Pakistan lost its eastern territory in 1971, what is today an independent Muslim majority country, Bangladesh.

India is the world's largest democracy with a robust system of rule of law, civil liberties, and religious freedom. Though India is the birthplace of many religions, its political core reflects a secular framework. The Indian polity consists of a multiparty federal republic with a parliamentary form of government headed by a Prime Minister. A President functions as the head of state and the legislature consists of the Lok Sabha (House of the People) and the Rajya Sabha (Council of States). As many as 28 States and 7 Union Territories are integral parts of the Indian Union and are governed, respectively, by Chief Ministers and Lieutenant Governors. Similar to the United States, three main branches of government—legislative, executive, and judiciary—function with separation of powers. The Judiciary, headed by the Supreme Court of India, ensures proper compliance by the other two branches through being vested with the final power of interpreting the Indian Constitution.

Currently, the more liberal, secular Congress Party and its allies, what is known as the United Progressive Alliance (UPA), holds the majority and began its second 5-year term in 2009 headed by Prime Minister Manmohan Singh. The more conservative Hindu Bhartiya Janata Party (BJP), which ruled India with its allies by forming the National Democratic Alliance from 1999–2004, is the main opposition party in the Parliament. Most of the Indian states are under the rule of the Congress Party. A few states are headed by the BJP, its allies, and some regional political outfits, while the Communist Party currently controls the states of Kerala, West Bengal, and Tripura. The Election Commission of India oversees an event in which over 700 million voters cast their votes through digital electronic voting machines (EVMs) through the massive deployment of election experts, administrators, police, and paramilitary personnel.

Governing powers and ruling parties greatly shape many of the cultural elements that in some eras were state-supported, while in other times were replaced or suppressed. Currently under the Congress Party, many government-sponsored programs provide funding and other resources to support pan-Indian and local cultural aspects—from the preservation of monuments to craft emporiums and performing arts festivals. Even though the government and funding that it provides is under the auspices of a secular model, much of Indian culture is connected to various religious aspects. Many of the ingredients chosen to discuss in this book exemplify this very quality of inseparability between culture and religion within the context of business.

Religion

Religion overwhelmingly defines India and many facets of its culture. India is home to several religions and is renowned for its spiritual centers, religious teachers, and yoga gurus. Buddhism and Jainism grew in India in the sixth century B.C.E. in connection with other internal Hindu reforms, reflecting a growing shift away from priestly authority over the ritual of fire sacrifice and toward individual forms of asceticism and philosophical speculation. Emperor Ashoka embraced Buddhist tenets and helped spread it to different parts of the world, starting with the country now known as Sri Lanka. The majority of Indians, according to the 2001 census, are Hindu (80.5%) and follow a wide variety of practices, as there is no single founder, central authority, or primary scripture to which all Hindus adhere. Modern Hinduism is marked by devotional practices to a pantheon of gods and goddesses, study of scriptures such as the *Bhagavad Gita* (Song of the Lord), performances of the epics and stories of god-heroes, and a variety of temple, domestic, and pilgrimage practices. About 13.4 percent of Indians are Muslims of Sunni and Shi'ite branches, most of which are strongly influenced by pervasive Sufi practices focused around a master teacher and their lineage. Musical expressions of poetry and pilgrimage to the tombs of saints known for their healing efficacy are common Sufi traditions in South Asian Islam. India is home to several world famous mausoleums, mosques, and historical monuments built during the Delhi Sultanate and Mughal rule: Qutub Minar, Lodhi Gardens, Taj Mahal, Jama Masjid, Lal Qila, Agra Fort, and Fatehpur Sikri are some of the well-known heritage buildings and are immensely popular with tourists. The British have left a legacy of colonial buildings and churches, many of which house convent schools that continue to undergird the early to late adolescent education system today. India is also home to several other minority groups such as Sikhs, Buddhists, Jains, Christians, Zoroastrians (Parsis), Jews, and others.[2]

Language

India is host to an astonishing number of languages and hundreds of dialects across its diverse landscape. There are currently 22 official languages recognized in the 8th Schedule of the Indian Constitution. Hindi is the most widely spoken of these official languages. Dravidian languages are spoken in southern provinces and a variety of vernacular languages are used in other provinces. However, English acquires a pride of place as it dominates in business and is the preferred medium of instruction for higher studies in technology and medicine. The emergence of India as the favorite business process outsourcing (BPO) and information technology (IT) services destination of global corporations has added to the popularity of English language across the country. Since English is the preeminent medium of the Internet and Web-based world, knowledge and fluency in English is considered a perfect launching pad for a good career and an important key to prosperity and wealth among millions of Indian youth and a burgeoning middle class.

Family and Societal Values

Indian society is family oriented and collectivistic where emphasis is on harmony and conformity with established cultural norms, social values, and family traditions. Elders command deep respect and family is a priority. Traditionally, individuals who are self-oriented were viewed with distrust, although with the changing socioeconomic conditions and growing disposable income, young professional Indians have started to indulge in a culture of consumption. A long-term relationship is the centerpiece of core Indian values and is the coveted goal of everyone from newspaper vendors to business tycoons and industrial houses. Traditionally family run businesses, such as the house of Tata, Birla, Goenka, Bajaj, and others, have dominated the Indian industrial landscape since the early 20th century. Many new powerhouses to emerge on the scene in recent years, including business ventures headed by the Ambani, Mittal, and Ruia families, along with Wipro, TCS, and Infosys, are more often than not either family run conglomerations, offshoots of such businesses, or started by close friends and associates where a history of positive long-term interactions is valued highly alongside business skills.

Food and Dress

Food and dress are central to Indian culture. Legends about the Roman Empire's depletion of gold and wealth for the love of exotic Indian textiles are well known. Adventure voyages of European sailors in search of a sea route to India to gain access to its aromatic spices are part of both folklore and historical chronicles. Probably because of its long-term affiliation with important trading routes among many nations and its fabulous wealth of resources, India boasts a wide assortment of products. A variety of cuisines were developed based on local ingredients and raw materials as well as food items introduced into India from trading adventures in distant lands. Most contemporary Indian food is made with some form of curry, a blend of strong aromatic spices that has many regional and dish-specific versions. Each and every region has some kind of special regional cuisine to offer based on a unique concoction of local spices and herbs, from Hyderabad's mutton and chicken *biryanis* (rice pilaf) to the coconut infused stews of Kerala. Vegetarianism is widely prevalent in the south and west, while the north and east relish a wide variety of nonvegetarian meals of fish, seafood, lamb, goat, and eggs. Beef is taboo among many upper-caste Hindus and many Muslims don't eat pork. Rice is a staple food in southern and eastern India, while wheat-based breads occupy a primary spot in the dietary preferences in north and central India. Different types of lentils form the basis for many standard main dishes. Milk-based products and sweets are popular throughout the country, each region having its own specialty.

India is known for its range of colorful fabrics, embroidery, and tapestry designs. Indians utilize a huge diversity of materials and designs for both daily use and special occasions. Western forms of dress are immensely popular in business and formal settings, keeping in mind modifications based on climate. While men in business routinely wear shirts, trousers, and suits with ties, women will wear a mix of *salwaar* suits (long tunic top and pants), Western wear, and saris, depending on the corporate culture. The sari is still the most distinctive women's apparel in India and is available in all kinds of fabrics and designs, including the "career woman's" no-iron choice of polyester blends. Indian women also prefer mostly gold jewelry, although certain regions also favor silver and certain gemstones. Regional ethnic dress for men and women reflect local influences and availability, weather, ritual roles, and textile specialties.

Festivals

A variety of festivals throughout the year grace the length and breadth of India. Most of the festivals are directly or indirectly linked with religion and agriculture and are celebrated in spring (January through April) and after monsoon seasons (August through November). Spring festivals mark the conclusion of the winter agricultural season and the beginning of summer. Post-monsoon festivals correspond with harvest time and the beginning of the winter season. The Hindu festival cycle that marks special events from religious (mythological) history and birthdays or special days of the gods are predominant in the annual calendar, including Holi, Navaratri, and Diwali, the Festival of Lights. Every major religion adds their own holidays that are recognized on a national level. For Muslims, big festivals include Ramadan, culminating in the feast of Id-ul-fitr, Muharram, and Bakr-id. Christmas is a national holiday and is celebrated in hundreds of cities and towns across the country. Similarly, there are religious festivals for Sikhs, Buddhists, Jains, Jews, and others.

Music and Dance

India's performing arts combine both music and dance. The range of performance arts, genres, and styles is enormous—yet globalization of mass media, changing tastes, new technology, and new styles are profoundly transforming them. Classical, folk, and contemporary forms are constantly being revised and reformulated in conversation (and sometimes tension) between aspects of tradition and innovation. Performing arts arose out of and were shaped in many religious and secular contexts, including temples, royal courts, town storytellers, and the wandering poet-saints of India. There is also a hallowed tradition of teacher-student relationships in India, as dancers and musicians traditionally apprentice with a master artist for many years, although institutions, some of them government supported, have become popular training grounds for fine arts and crafts. Each region has its own unique dance styles and preferences in musical instruments. Bharata Natyam, Kathak, Odissi, Kuchipudi, and Kathakali are well-known classical dance styles, many of which have come to represent Indian culture in the larger diaspora. Sitar, veena, and tabla are the most recognizable imports in Indian music, even though there is a diverse range of both string and percussion instruments. The Mumbai film industry, known around the world as Bollywood, also wields enormous influence on popular performing arts through song and dance sequences in films and TV shows.

It is worth noting that continuity and diversity are paramount in almost all walks of Indian life. Many traditions are several centuries old, but still in vogue, while many others have evolved from interaction and assimilation of several other cultures and traditions that came with the migratory populations or conquests from the north. Many of these arts have morphed from foreign into native forms over India's long history of trade and friendly relations with neighboring as well as far-off countries.

Rise of the Elephant

Historically, India has existed in the imagination of many as an "El Dorado"—a place known for its textiles, spices, and gems that represented a wealth that intrigued adventurers, explorers, and even marauders, upon occasion. Over the course of millennia, fluctuations in power and control, both internally and externally, left what would eventually become the nation state of India with a mixed legacy of political, financial, and social problems to resolve. After gaining independence in 1947, India chose to pursue a very cautious socialistic economic policy that was focused on self-reliance and provided protection to indigenous business. This model, known as a mixed economy, where government controlled the majority of industries and financial services while allowing a private sector to coexist in select ventures, continued until 1990. The average rate during this period recorded low growth from 3 to 4 percent in GDP, also known as the "Hindu Rate of Growth."

But in 1991, an empty treasury and a near bankruptcy forced the Indian government to introspectively revaluate its economic policy.

More out of desperation than that of a planned strategic shift, the Indian government liberalized its economic policy, embraced globalization, and triggered a 180 degree turn by ushering in an era of reform that removed most of the restrictions on business. Since then, India has been registering a healthy growth rate from 6 to 8 percent, and after China, is the second fastest growing market in the world. India is undergoing a rapid globalization of its economy and foreign investments in the country are on the rise as more and more opportunities for business and partnerships are opening up. In less than two decades since the economic reforms of 1991, India has emerged as a champion exporter of services, ranging from computer software to back office work, call centers, and research and development (R&D).

A key factor supporting this economic growth has been the interplay of technology and changing world circumstances that started the flattening process described so well by Thomas Friedman in his 2005 book, *The World Is Flat*, which opened up unprecedented opportunities for India. These opportunities were neither conceived nor imagined by India's planners, bureaucrats, or businesses, but a series of sequential events catapulted India to the forefront in a partnership with the United States and the world unlike any other time in its history.

The basis for this partnership between India and the United States began when thousands of programmers from India, who scored high in technical abilities and English language proficiency, arrived in the United States in the early to mid-1990s to fix the Y2K bug: to reprogram a glitch in the formatting of the date from MMYYDD to MMYYDDDD. Without this shift, on January 1, 2000, corrupt data files would set off a chain reaction wiping out bank accounts, compromising national security and intelligence capabilities, among other systemwide repercussions.

Information technology also started changing its gears around 1995, as Friedman notes, when the arrival of the first Internet browser, Netscape, broadened the reach and attraction of the nascent technological wonder, the Internet, beyond e-mails and ushered in a worldwide Web revolution. Ability to access the Internet by any computer with a modem from anywhere sparked the imagination of smart technology and business minds and led to an unprecedented spurt in online businesses all over the world in a very short time period, the so-called dot-com boom of the late 1990s. The United States led the euphoria of this boom, which led to billions of dollars of investments in broadband global connectivity through satellites and undersea cables. Better computer processing power and steady decline in storage prices fed this boom to create a huge bubble in the stock market that ingloriously burst at the turn of the century.[3]

However, the convergence of ever growing processing power, declining storage prices, and around the clock seamless broadband connectivity proved to be a boon in disguise for India and its emerging IT companies. Many of the Y2K returnees kept in touch with their U.S. contacts and had started working in India's emerging IT sector. Their availability and ready willingness to work at 1/10th or lower wages along with an average 10–12 hour time differential encouraged several U.S. corporations to explore outsourcing of software development, customer service, and other routine work to India. At the time, the United States was struggling with high costs in a depressed market and terabytes of idle bandwidth capacity. One project led to many and started a mad rush to partner with Indian IT companies, which made themselves available 24/7, 365 days a year, for various outsourced services. Thus began the saga of U.S. partnership with India and its emerging IT sector and a new face of globalization in a virtual world where local geography started to lose its relevance.

Business Opportunities in India

Indian dominance in Call Center, BPO, and other IT-enabled services has prompted hundreds of U.S. and European corporations to slice up their services segments and outsource them to IT services companies or business partners in India to take advantage of cost arbitrage and stay competitive. However, now as India is getting richer and its market is expanding, several global corporations are relocating their R&D and other high-end services in the value chain to India to develop new products and services that they plan to market to their existing clients in the United States and Europe, as well as to local customers in India, China, and other emerging markets. The writing on the wall is clear: get ready to witness a fierce battle among multinational companies (MNCs) and Indian companies for market share and customers.

Along with China, India is the world's second fastest growing economy registering unprecedented growth since economic liberalization in 1991. It is poised to grow at more than 7% in its current fiscal year ending in March 2010 according to Dr. C. Rangarajan, who heads the Indian Prime Minister's Economic Advisory Council (EAC).[4] According to the Economic Survey 2009–2010, net capital flows saw an impressive growth at US$29.6 billion in April–September 2009 from US$12 billion for the previous year; foreign exchange reserves increased by US$31.5 billion and stood at US$283.5 billion in December 2009; that is, a 12 percent growth in the nine-month period from US$252 billion by end of March 2009. From a meager 54.6 million telephone subscribers in 2003, the number increased to 562 million as of October 31, 2009, catapulting India into the second fastest growing market after China for telecommunication products and services.[5] These examples are just a few of the many markers of a thriving business economy.

We are witnessing a major change in business thinking. Cisco Systems relocated its globalization planning along with its head honcho to Bangalore in 2007, following in the footsteps of IBM, GE, Accenture, and others. These corporations have put into effect an Asian shift in their strategic plan to stay close to emerging markets and consumers, to leverage the superior technical abilities of Indian engineers and graduates in product design and innovation, and to neutralize the advantages of Indian IT companies that are fast spreading their footprints all over the world.

India offers plenty of exciting business opportunities in almost every sector of the economy. These opportunities can be broadly summarized under the following categories.

Services

The services sector brought India on to the drawing boards of business strategists and planners of multinational corporations all over the world. A small beginning that started with the collaboration of Indian IT companies and programmers in software development and code writing has become a multibillion dollar industry. Call center management to routine business processing work nurtured this sector and enhanced its attractiveness by building on the strength of India's technical prowess and the professionalism of its IT services companies. Today this sector boasts an enviable list of clients in the United States and Europe who are working with Indian companies and their technical whiz kids on retooling their companies to remain lean and competitive.

U.S. IT services giants GE, IBM, Accenture, and Cisco Systems continue to increase their footprints in India not only through vigorous campus hiring, employee training, and retention strategies, but also have been open to local acquisitions such as Daksh and Mphasis by IBM and EDS (acquired by HP in 2008 for $13.9 billion), respectively, to name a few. Dell is aggressively pursuing Perot Systems in order to enter into the lucrative IT services industries.[6] Top Indian companies such as TCS, Infosys, and Wipro are following similar strategies. Besides a near pan-India presence, these Indian corporations have been aggressively expanding their networks by opening more offices not only in the United States, Europe, and Australia, where most of their clients are based, but also in China, Hong Kong, Singapore, and other Far East locations to explore emerging business prospects.

Outside the familiar IT/BPO/KPO (knowledge processing outsourcing) services there are immense opportunities in telecommunication, banking, insurance, finance, media and mass communication, and several other service centered businesses.

Infrastructure

India is seriously deficient in its infrastructure capabilities. The government has embarked on ambitious infrastructure projects and is building modern highways, bridges, cargo ports, airports, and power plants. It is modernizing its transport systems in major cities through subways and city buses. Emphasis is on eco-friendly construction, cost-efficiency, and expansion of alternative, sustainable, and green technologies. Most of the infrastructure projects are being executed under a public-private partnership (PPP) model. The opportunities in the infrastructure sector can be divided under the following categories:

1. Highways: National Highways Authority of India (NHAI) spearheads a network of highways crisscrossing the country. The Golden Quadrilateral, connecting the four super metros—Mumbai, Delhi, Kolkata, and Chennai—and the East-West Corridor are the two major projects being constructed by some of the best construction companies and infrastructural giants in the world, including Bouygues of France, Hong Kong based China Harbor & Bridge Company, Laing O'Rourke of the UK, South Korea's Hyundai Engineering and Construction, Thailand's Italthai Engineering, Sweden's Skanska, Dyckerhoff of Russia, Widmann from Germany, Malaysia's IJM Construction, and Japan's Kajima and Taisei, to name a few.
2. Railways: India has the second largest railway network after Russia in the world. But much of the network is old and reaching the end of its life. Indian Railways has started modernizing its network, stations, and services. Dedicated rail freight corridors—the

Eastern Corridor connecting Delhi with Howrah and the Western Corridor between Mumbai and Delhi—are being built for efficient cargo transport. Several cities are building local suburban railway networks. Although India built its first suburban railway in Kolkata in the 1980s, Delhi Metro (DMRC) is the first world-class mass rapid transit project undertaken in the country. Launched in December 2002, the project is on an ambitious trajectory to complete a 120 KM long network before the Commonwealth Games in October 2010. This truly international collaboration includes the participation of Itochu Corporation, Kumagai Gumi Co. Ltd, Shimizu Corporation, and Mitsubishi Corporation from Japan; Skanska International Civil Engineering AB from Sweden; Dyckerhoff & Widmann AG, Germany; Samsung Corporation and KOROS based in Korea; and Alstom Transport SA and Alcatel CGA Transport from France.

3. Ports: Most of the Indian ports are proving to be inadequate to meet the demands of ever increasing cargo traffic to and from India. Government has identified hundreds of ports for modernization and capacity expansion. Companies from all over the globe are opening offices in India, looking to bring technology, investment, products, and services to India's maritime sector.[7]

4. Airports: Modernization and upgrades of existing airports and construction of new airports under a PPP model has opened up opportunities for domestic and international construction majors. Modernization of Delhi and Mumbai airports is currently in process and are operated and managed by joint venture companies DIAL (Delhi International Airport Private Limited), a consortium of companies led by GMR Group, and MIAL (Mumbai International Airport Private Limited) by that of GVK Group. New airports have been constructed in Bangalore and Hyderabad, the latter with Zurich Airport as a major stakeholder. A consortium company, BIAL, which is owned by Siemens Project Ventures, Zurich Airport, GVK Group, and Karnataka State Government, along with a few other Indian companies, manages the Bangalore airport.[8] The government also plans to construct several airports in nonmetro cities across the country.

5. Power: Inadequacy of power availability and poor management of generation and transmission have been keeping India from speeding up its reforms. As the Indian economy continues to grow, its power sector has been trying to keep pace with the growth rate. The demand for power is growing exponentially

and the scope of growth of this sector is immense. Business opportunities exist in thermal, hydel, nuclear power, and even in renewable energy sources. Several international companies such as ABB, GE, Siemens AG, Enron, and Bechtel work closely with Indian power majors BHEL, NTPC, NHPC, State Electricity Boards, and other domestic power organizations.

Manufacturing

It is commonplace to find a "Made in India" label on Banana Republic shirts or Nike sneakers found in U.S. stores and outlets. In general, India manufactures a wide range of products from apparel, sporting goods, automotive parts, precision machinery, and gemstones to cars, trucks, and high-tech engineering goods for a variety of companies. Along with China, it is fast emerging as a global manufacturing hub. For example, Delhi-Gurgaon has served as the primary automobile manufacturing site for Suzuki and Hero Honda. In recent years, Chennai has also emerged as a major manufacturing hub for automobiles (Ford, Hyundai, BMW) and trucks (Ashok Leyland, Renault-Nissan, Dailmer). Lately, Chennai has also been attracting electronics companies (Nokia, Alcatel-Lucent, Ericsson) to set up manufacturing bases. India has all the requisite skills in product, process and capital engineering, and quality management. India's cheap, skilled manpower is attracting a number of companies that span a diverse number of industries, further increasing India's role as a global manufacturing powerhouse.

Mining and Metallurgy

India is rich in natural resources, but extraction and processing of mineral ores are primitive by world standards. The government is removing regulations and restrictions in order to attract global companies and investment in the latest technologies. Caterpillar of the United States, Komatsu of Japan and several other leading international companies are actively working in the Indian mining sector.

Agriculture

Agriculture is the mainstay for a large section of the Indian population, but still depends on the vagaries of monsoon seasons and archaic methods of cultivation. But now efforts are being directed toward an integrated development of agriculture through expansion of irrigation, mechanization, research in agro-biotechnology, genetic engineering, and other activities to expand food grain production and improve productivity. The food-processing sector is garnering increased attention and has the potential to become a growth driver for the economy. Cargill, Monsanto, General Mills, and Kellogg are some of the international companies active in the Indian food and agriculture sector. Kraft Foods Inc., the world's second biggest processed food company, is getting ready to enter India through its $18.9 billion buyout of the UK-based Cadbury, a company that has national presence and excellent brand awareness in the Indian market.[9]

Other Opportunities

Besides the above core sectors, India offers immense possibilities for investment and collaboration in many other areas, including:

Education: The government has embarked on a reform agenda to improve standards of school and higher education. Work is being done to streamline regulatory bodies and usher in a more integrated and improved curriculum. For example, the Indian government has cleared the Foreign Educational Institutions Bill.[10] Once passed by Parliament, such a bill would allow foreign universities to open remote campuses in India, which in turn will significantly impact the quality of higher education and research in the country. Harvard Business School has already set up an Indian Research Center (IRC) in Mumbai,[11] and several universities in the United States and the UK are increasingly collaborating with the Indian School of Business (ISB), Hyderabad, IIMs, and other reputed institutions in order to create synergetic opportunities in the field of education, research, and technology.

Health Care: Access to affordable health care remains a challenge for a majority of Indians, more so to those who live in small towns and villages where hospitals are either not available or are poorly staffed with little or no services. Several specialty hospitals in foreign collaboration are already working in several cities in India. Apollo Hospitals, Max Healthcare, and Fortis Healthcare are a few of the big names in India's burgeoning health care industry.

Media and Entertainment: India is home to the largest film industry in the world that churns out hundreds of films a year in several languages and local dialects. The recent success of Danny Boyle's Indian theme based film, *Slumdog Millionaire*, and its eight Oscar wins have further raised the awareness of the Indian film industry popularly known as "Bollywood" in Hollywood studios and among the LA film celebrity circuit. Director Stephen Spielberg's Dreamworks Studios has joined hands with Anil Ambani's Reliance Big Entertainment, which is just the beginning of many more partnerships in the cinematic and allied industries.

Hospitality and Tourism: The entire country of India has less than 140,000 hotel rooms, which is close to the number of rooms available in the single U.S. city of Las Vegas, Nevada.[12] With its growing economy and rising income, India is likely to see a sizeable jump in business executive traffic and in the number of domestic and international tourists. International hotel chains, including Marriot, Hyatt, and Hilton, have been doing business in India for many years, but India is seriously deficient in hotel rooms, convention centers, and other such infrastructure to meet growing demands. In connection, there are tremendous opportunities for theme-based parks, water sports, and adventure tourism in the country.

Medical Tourism: India has emerged as a favored destination for expensive high-end surgeries built on the reputation of its excellent surgeons and cost differential. A huge gap between treatment costs in the United States and Europe and those at world-class hospitals in India, in addition to insurance gaps, has opened up opportunities. Patients fly to India, where they can get their treatment at a much lower cost, and have the bonus of visiting and enjoying their time in India. For example, Medanta, a self-titled "medicity" with a multispecialty hospital in Gurgaon, is taking the lead in attracting foreign clientele. Headed by renowned cardiologist, Dr. Naresh Trehan, it offers state of the art treatment facilities and patient care infrastructure.

A Note on Business Opportunities in India

It is pertinent to note that when it comes to business opportunities in India there is no other word that describes it better than "diversity." India is the world's largest democracy and home to the world's largest middle class (about 250–300 million). India is really a tale of two Indias, the relationship between the two yet to be fully determined.

The first is a primarily urban India marked by rising incomes and people with aspirations who are ready to embark on the path of consumption. The second is a predominantly rural India where literacy is low and income levels are slowly increasing, but dreams of good things in life and incentives have been introduced to support entrepreneurial and innovative work that will create uplift among the economically downtrodden. The statistics on poverty are widely varying, ranging from 27.5 to 54.8 percent based on different key factors, and national per capita income hovers around $1,000 a year.[13] At the same time, there are pockets of affluence concentrated in metro cities and sporadically distributed around the country that can be compared to the rich social segments in any developed country. Their consumption levels are skyrocketing and can be witnessed by the presence of increasing luxury brands entering the Indian market in recent years from Porsche cars to Louis Vuitton bags. India will be continuing to work out the relationship between these two India-s, both of which have tremendous potential.

The opportunities and challenges for American businesses in India lie in mastering the knowledge of market and consumer segments based on their incomes, aspirations, and preferences and then developing appropriate products and services catering to these customers. These challenges can be addressed better by partnering with Indian companies and working with Indian executives and by developing a work environment that fosters trust, understanding, and appreciation of Indian cultural norms, as well as personal and social sensitivities.

Chapter 2

A Recipe for Business Success: The Most Important Ingredients

In scanning the vast diversity of Indian culture, there are several features that stand out as being vital for those engaged in business enterprises in South Asia. This chapter gives a synopsis of the 11 ingredients we have identified as the most helpful for creating a strong, adaptable foundation for negotiating business interactions in South Asia. We start by providing a few overall notes about these ingredients, before describing each one in turn.

First, the ingredients are mostly drawn from the religious and cultural traditions of the majority population in India: Hinduism. This is a choice based on the impact of these ingredients to explain the mindset, expectations, and behaviors encountered in South Asia. To a somewhat lesser degree, American mindsets also require a certain degree of fluency in cultural aspects originating from the predominant Judeo-Christian religious worldviews, even though the population of the United States is one of the most diverse in the world. Religion cannot be ignored for its immense influence on cultural norms no matter where you are.

Many of the cultural ingredients in this book have been adopted more widely in India, and would not necessarily be considered *only* Hindu in origin or practice today. For example, the caste system, a hierarchical ordering of society that is Hindu in origin, is also found among other Indian Muslim and Christian communities. As business environments are composed of people from many different religious backgrounds, an effort has been made to mention the range of influence across the population. Any appropriate correlating ideas from other religious backgrounds are mentioned in brief within each chapter. In all cases, each of the 11 would be recognizable to most people of South Asian origin.

Second, each of these ingredients isolates a particular cultural feature. In practice, many of these ingredients work together and cannot be separated. Our understanding is that if you become familiar with the cultural aspects that are the most prominent, you will be able to recognize their effects more readily in different business situations. It is a way of becoming familiar with the most often utilized spices individually, understanding their flavors and properties before being able to understand what is mixed together to produce the overall flavor of the entire dish.

Third, the core mission of this book is to translate the influence of these ingredients as immediately and clearly as possible into business contexts. This focus inherently requires more background information than a simple list of etiquette rules, and less information than a book on Indian history, culture, and religion. To find that balance, we explain the main word and concept, placing it in its most widely recognized contexts with as little jargon or foreign subconcepts as possible for the sake of accessibility to a wide audience. To prevent oversimplification, we include references for further information on the topic for those who are interested.

And a final note based on the question: Why 11 ingredients? In many American settings, the magic number is usually "10" as reflected in the propensity toward making top 10 lists. This is indicative of an American way of summarizing important information in bullet point format. In Indian contexts, ending on the 10, 50, 100, 1,000, and so on (i.e., any whole number with a zero at the end), is considered complete within itself. When people give donations, they always add +1 to the amount (e.g., $10 + 1 = 11$, $50 + 1 = 51$, $100 + 1 = 101$). The cultural reason behind the practice of +1 is that it creates a gesture of extension that invites more exchange to occur, more money and abundance, more gifts, and more reciprocity. It is symbolic of giving that little extra without being asked, creating a token debt of sorts that will eventually be repaid in kind.

In our own list of 10 + 1, we acknowledge the cultural practice in order to suggest that extra extension of a person when they land in a foreign situation as they adopt new strategies for better interactions. The 10 + 1 also indicates the continuation of the list indefinitely—we are marking the most important cultural ingredients, but depending on context and type of business interaction, there are many other ingredients that could be useful. The appendix outlines what some of these extended ingredient lists might look like in different regions. We propose the list that follows as a good, solid beginning.

A Recipe for Business Success: The Most Important Ingredients 21

Ingredient 1: Hospitality

Hindu practices of devotion are the most widespread, overlooked cultural model for conducting business in India. At the center of this chapter are the four main elements of *puja* (worship): greeting, offerings, exchange, and reciprocity. As a means to create and sustain a relationship between humans and gods, puja relies on a grammar of hospitality. A proper welcome, the giving and receiving of appropriate gifts, and other types of exchanges between devotees and gods start a cycle of reciprocity. The actions of puja are replicated in other contexts—including business—to set up and support a strong ongoing relationship between two or more parties. By utilizing puja as a template, you will be able to understand your role as guest, understand expectations, and utilize the grammar of hospitality to guide your participation in building solid business partnerships.

Ingredient 2: Role Expectations

Dharma (duty) dictates the responsibilities of a person based on the various roles one plays in life. An understanding of dharma in the context of business helps identify the roles and expected actions of everyone from the CEO and manager down to the team players in a company. Dharma that is connected to individual roles works in alignment with a higher sense of ethical responsibility and mission of the company. These two forms of dharma—the dharma of individual roles and the dharma of mission—are inseparably intertwined and have lasting repercussions in the way people approach their jobs. This chapter also covers what is expected of Western businesspeople in various contexts as they enter into business partnerships within this system.

Ingredient 3: Business Caste or Hierarchy

Businesses have their own innate systems of hierarchy that take certain cues from family history and dynamics. To distinguish and mind the lines of power, a respect for the system opens up access to information that is in the hands of different levels of authority. Minding the lines of power works better than barging in and demanding information from those of higher rank. Through developing a sense for the workings of caste in Indian business, you will be able to identify and map out the relevant network of relationships to determine who to approach to produce the most efficient results.

Ingredient 4: Project Process and Management

Pilgrimage, undertaken by people from many different religious traditions in India, offers an insightful model for understanding the course and completion of any project implemented within an Indian company. Paying attention to the different steps—from the first intention and clarification of the project and preparation, community building and "rest stops," and also carrying forward knowledge gained into new projects, the features of pilgrimage structure a project for success. By learning to see a project as a form of pilgrimage, businesspeople can see what people expect from it and how to reach a successful conclusion.

Ingredient 5: Leadership and Teamwork

The "one and the many" is a common phrase that describes the religious and political pluralities of India. In business, this idea translates into the ability to lead and create team cohesion through seeing each part and person as being unique, but also as participants working within and toward a singular, unified vision or goal. Leaders are defined by creating spaces for leadership qualities to emerge from within the team and fostering joint ownership of projects.

Ingredient 6: Risk and Action

Karma yoga, defined as action without attachment to the outcomes, arises out of one of the most influential writings in India, the *Bhagavad Gita*. While businesspeople often focus single-mindedly on achieving particular outcomes, business leaders in India incorporate the principles of karma yoga in three ways: through specific risk-taking strategies, a focus on what is "right" action (rather than the reward), and a strong philanthropic impulse. Understanding this can improve the success rate of business initiatives in India.

Ingredient 7: The Pursuit of Wealth

Underlying Indian culture is a religiously sanctified right to the pursuit of pleasure, wealth, and success. In particular, the pursuit of wealth (*artha*) frames business as part of the religious sphere, rather than in opposition to or outside of it. Preferences toward certain types of investments and savings, practices of philanthropy, and newfound earning potential and entrepreneurial incentives arise out of Indian perceptions about the origins and uses for prosperity. This chapter compares and contrasts Indian attitudes toward moneymaking with the cultural and religious attitudes toward wealth found in the United States.

Ingredient 8: The Original Business Contract

In the ancient practice of fire sacrifice, the proper performance of words and actions created a binding, nonnegotiable contract with the gods. Intermediaries are crucial to setting up a context of efficacious exchange and compliance. In modern times, the practice of sacrifice translates into a template for understanding contract negotiations, appropriate execution of offers, and final expectations for all parties involved.

Ingredient 9: Nonconfrontational Negotiation

The idea of nonviolence, or *ahimsa*, pervades much of Indian culture. A negotiating approach that follows the path of least resistance and minimizes harm to all involved succeeds best. Ahimsa affects each of the questions of context—from how you view *who* you are negotiating with, *when* and *where*, to *how* you approach your partners and colleagues. Intimidation does not work well in the process of shaping the *what* and *why* of negotiation—building relationships and shared goals. Learning how to recognize and utilize this ingredient will smooth the process of negotiation and prevent misinterpretations.

Ingredient 10: Cultural Views of Time and Space

From IST (Indian Stretched Time) and the notion of the "right time" to start a task, to the placement of people in a meeting and treatment of office space, cultural notions of time and space influence the rhythms and environments of business. A familiarity with these aspects prevents undue frustrations.

Ingredient 11: Women in the Workplace

Gender dynamics are changing fast in India as young, educated women lead the workforce in certain industries and become in some cases the primary financial support for entire families. In business contexts, the growing presence of independent, unchaperoned women raises issues of appropriate social and physical interaction that this chapter will address. While harassment and gender bias exist to various degrees, career women draw on a range of culture based models to strengthen their roles as leaders and managers in the workforce. Both male and female managers will benefit from this exploration of some of the primary gender-based issues that may influence your professional interactions.

Chapter 3

Ingredient 1: Hospitality

Location: New Delhi, India; Corporate Headquarters of a Japanese Corporation
Occasion: Visit of Chairman of the company's Singapore Regional HQ, Mr. Tanaka

It is a chilly winter morning in January as the entire staff prepares for the arrival of the VIP guest. The outer walls had just received a coat of fresh paint and flowers arranged in decorative formations adorn the front office. From the front door to the entrance area, workers roll out a welcoming red carpet. Inside the office everything looks impeccably sharp. Senior managers to errand runners come to work dressed in crisp attire and are well groomed for the special occasion. When Mr. Tanaka arrives, the India office chief escorts him from his car to the reception area. A female employee in traditional Indian clothing—colorful silk sari, henna designs on her hands, black kohl lining her eyes, and wearing beautiful gold jewelry and a red dot on her forehead—applies the auspicious red paste tilak *on his forehead. She then places a marigold and rose garland around his neck and bows with folded hands to complete the gesture of welcoming him. Surrounded by senior managers, the guest is ushered into the company's large conference room and introduced to the staff as fresh fruit, snacks, and beverages are served. Conversation centers on Mr. Tanaka's flight, hotel, weather, comfort, and inconveniences, if any. Nearly an hour goes by in attentive conversational exchange and expressions of gratitude for the honor of hosting Mr. Tanaka at the Delhi office before the "business" meeting begins.*

The warmth of Indian hospitality is legendary. No matter what your position in a company that has led you to visit India on business, a variation of this "red carpet" treatment awaits you. As you arrive at the

26 Inside the Indian Business Mind

Flower garlands, sold for *pujas*, marriages, and formal greetings for VIPs. (K. Zubko)

office for your first meeting, ready for business with your presentation materials, power point slides, charts, and a notepad, you might feel overwhelmed, suspicious, or embarrassed with all the fuss and attention to every aspect of your well-being. You might be wondering, even as you sip the hot tea that was brought and look at your watch, when the meeting you had shown up promptly for 20 minutes ago is going to start. In actuality, the meeting has begun, and these overtures of hospitality (fresh surroundings, greeting and gifting, food and drink, and polite conversation) are part of the required protocols to different degrees whenever you first meet up with anybody, whether in someone's home or place of business in India.

It might astound you to know that hospitality is rooted, in part, in a key element of modern-day Hindu religious practice called puja, or "worship."[1] The actions of puja create and sustain relationships between people and their gods. Many of the same dynamics explain interactions between people that occur in contexts outside of religion, including business contexts. This chapter introduces puja as a model of hospitality in order to shed light on the expectations of receptivity, exchange, and reciprocity that comes along with your role as a guest of your Indian business associates. The general attitude of Indians toward their guests is very welcoming and accepting. They make every effort to put their guests at ease and indulge them with attention, food and drinks, give parting gifts, and request them to revisit soon. A foreign company and its representatives qualify as "guests" in the Indian ethos. Understanding the role of a guest within the template of puja helps you to adapt your behavior to both domestic and business contexts and participate in the creation of strong working relationships with your business associates in India.

Puja

Even though the best English definition of puja is "worship," the intent and actions of puja are very different than Western notions of worship. Four main features define puja: greeting, offerings, exchange, and reciprocity (gift giving).

Greeting

In the Hindu worldview, the divine appears in the world in many ways. Gods dwell in temples and homes in stone and brass statues, in nature in the form of rivers, mountains, and stones, and in saintly people and gurus (teachers). The divine permanently resides in any of these forms, or appears temporarily in order to bless those present. No matter whether a permanent or temporary appearance, it is appropriate protocol to greet the divine for making itself present before the person. It is the first action performed—the welcoming of the presence of the divine. This is usually done through placing the palms of the hands together in prayer position, or *namaste* (I honor you), or through the touching of the feet in the Hindu tradition. This action welcomes the divine.

Already you might be thinking, "What does this have to do with me? I am not a god." Much to your surprise, this is not exactly true. There is an ancient understanding that all guests, even business associates, are to be treated as well as gods—*"atithi devo bhava"* (Guest is like God).[2] Gods show up often as guests or even beggars (in disguise) at people's homes in many of the myths of the religions of India. These narratives suggest that the person that has arrived at the doorstep as a guest should be treated *as if* they were a possible divine visitor. Even though guests are not literal gods, the belief in exemplary generosity and conduct toward guests has been instilled in the Indian psyche for generations and is practiced by Indians of practically all descriptions irrespective of their class, caste, religion, or social standing.

When people meet, a warm welcome is the first step. Usually Indians greet each other and their guests with folded hands with the word namaste, instead of a handshake, to acknowledge and welcome the divine in the other person. If the guest is a family elder, or an eminent person, the host/associate may greet him or her by touching their feet. It is common to greet parents, teachers, priests and other respectable elders by touching their feet in private or even in public settings. It portrays respect for age and wisdom and a sense of gratitude. While no one may bend to touch your feet, do not be surprised to see such actions around you in families, political arenas, and businesses. When you are greeted with namaste, it is customary to return the gesture back. This ritualized exchange of greetings marks acceptance and willing participation in your role as a VIP guest.

Offerings

After a proper greeting is conducted, the second part of a puja is the presentation of offerings. In the formal ritual texts, there are 16 primary offerings that can be given to the gods. These range from offering a seat, water to drink and to bathe, and food, to fresh adornments—flowers, perfume, jewelry, clothing—and entertainment such as singing and dancing. Not all of these are offered at every puja. In fact the offering of one's praise or a single flower is enough. Pujas vary from region to region, and can be very simple or very elaborate and last for days during festivals. Whatever is offered will be the best that person can afford at that time.

As a guest of the highest order, you will be offered something to drink and eat often and usually near the beginning of contact with your hosts or associates. This may happen at any time of the day or night that you arrive, while hosts may go out of their way to offer up the best of what they have. This is a sacrifice that hosts willingly place upon themselves. In continued deference to the guest, a host, after serving snacks or a meal, may or may not join the guest in taking something to eat. This is not because there may not be enough space or food for everyone but to show respect and attention to the guest in a gesture of personal sacrifice and to ensure his guest's complete satisfaction. If the guest relishes her meal and indulges in extra servings the host feels extremely happy and relieved that all the hard work and preparation has paid off. Many foreign visitors have erred by refusing a second helping—a mark of dissatisfaction in the eyes of the host, or commenting on the wastefulness of unwanted servings. Instead, if you are full, it is better to leave behind a small portion of your first serving, or welcome another smaller serving and leave a little on the plate.

Such food service practices are common and can be witnessed anywhere from dinner at someone's house to marriage ceremonies where hundreds of people are invited for community dinner. In a simple dinner at home, the host or more often the wife of the host prefers to eat after serving the guest, which can be unsettling for foreign visitors. During a marriage feast the bride's family members do not eat until everyone from the groom's side has finished eating because they are their guests. Sacrifice translates in essence to giving primacy to the invited guest (her time, attention, and comforts) and

Food and drink as forms of hospitality: a *thali* meal plate from South India and tea being served in an office meeting. (K. Zubko)

relegating the host's own priorities and inconveniences (her own meal, appointments, etc.) to second place.

Even when entering the conference room in India, drink and food will be the first order of business. In American settings, food is often sidelined to a buffet table to be nibbled on or to be eaten at the conclusion of the meeting. In a business lunch, small talk, if any, moves quickly on to projects, often before any food arrives at the table. The food first policy in India is so deeply rooted in notions of hospitality and the proper reception of a guest that trying to speed up the process may be considered an affront to the efforts of your host.

Other elaborate gifts or tokens also may be offered during a visit. For Mr. Tanaka, he was given a statue of a Hindu god and traditional sweets amidst short speeches indicating the great honor his visit has bestowed on the employees as part of his departure. The consistent stream of attention may create a feeling of unease with the extent of the offerings or the seeming inconvenience or bother you are causing your hosts/associates as they are running around preparing things for you. The elaborate nature of these offerings may even strike you as a form of flattery or bribery. While bribery does exist, dismiss these thoughts of suspicion or embarrassment. While your associates do hope to impress you and want your business, their actions are motivated primarily out of timeless cultural traditions. The best approach is to learn to graciously receive all of these offerings as part of business as usual.

Exchange

Out of all the possible offerings, the most important item presented at the height of the puja is the offering of light, or *aarti*. Traditionally this is a camphor flame, or a lit cotton wick fed by ghee (clarified butter) or sesame oil held in a small clay or brass lamp that is bestowed before the god. The offering of light illuminates every feature of the decorated god and introduces extra light that allows for a better viewing. The presentation of light highlights a third aspect of puja called *darshan*.

Harvard historian of religion Diana Eck defines darshan as "to see and be seen," a visual ritual exchange between the god and the worshipper.[3] This is not a one-sided viewing, in which only the worshipper sees the god. It is also believed that the god sees the worshipper. The introduction of light allows for this reciprocal viewing to occur under the best possible circumstances. When people decide to visit the gods in the temple they will typically call this "going for darshan." People bathe and dress in their finest clothes before going to temple or performing puja so that they may be viewed in the best light by the gods. It is a little like putting your best foot forward or wearing your Sunday best. The gods offer blessings and peace of mind in return.

The concept of darshan highlights the aspect of exchange that contributes to the building of all relationships with your Indian business associates and team members. As a guest in the homes and offices of your Indian colleagues, the host welcomes you and treats you to sumptuous food and delicacies with a sense of devotion and gratitude. Putting their best appearance forward, hosts aim to please their guests without fault. In return, the successful host accomplishes his objective of the guest's happiness and goodwill. The ultimate reward of this exchange for the host is in securing the complete satisfaction of the guest. For example, in the visit of Mr. Tanaka to the Indian branch office, lunch consisted of both Indian and Japanese foods. This was an effort on the part of the Indian associates to make sure Mr. Tanaka likes and is comfortable with the food, enjoys the experience, and is totally satisfied in the end, which is the real reward for the host. Mr. Tanaka's compliments actually complete the cycle of exchange.

The capital of satisfaction leads to profitable outcomes for both sides. In this cycle, satisfaction leads to new projects, bigger orders, and thank yous. In exchange, Indian companies and their associates continue to offer their highest quality products and the best of their resources and support. While this may look like customer satisfaction 101 in any country within which you may find yourself doing business, the pervasiveness of the puja model underscores the importance of exchange. A relationship that works along these lines of exchange promises success for all those involved.

Reciprocity

After light is offered to the gods, the light is brought back to the worshipper and given back as a blessing. It is symbolically taken into the hearts and eyes of the worshipper through fingertips that pass over the flame and are brought back to the eyes. The returning of offerings, as consecrated blessings, marks the fourth aspect of puja. It is not just light that is given back, but also offerings such as flowers and food.

In the end, the actions of puja come full circle. As a guest, there is an expectation to give something back in return, although any Indian host would vehemently deny this expectation directly. Gifting is an unstated protocol that is not discussed openly, as is the acceptable practice in the United States of asking the host/hostess what you can bring to an invited dinner or party. In India, reciprocal actions complete the relationship created, whether for the devotee and god through the process of puja, or for you and your business associates. There is a range of appropriate gifts that you can bring to present to your hosts, associates, and team members to fulfill the expectation of reciprocity on your part. Gifting appropriate items acknowledges the establishment of a relationship and indicates your continued willing participation in that relationship. Your actions signal an openness and an invitation to future exchanges. While all gifts are determined by context and relationship, a listing of some of the most common and appropriate gifts is given below:

- Stationary, pens (high quality), books
- Small electronic gadgets, clocks, desk calendars
- Items with insignia of the company
- Engraved items—paperweights, pens, etc.
- Plaques commemorating the visit/event
- Small decorative items

In general, avoid leather products and alcohol. Chocolate is a good idea, but depending on the season, can melt in transit. Whatever you give is only a token, and not meant to be a display of wealth, status, or competition. Gift wrapping is also favored no matter the size or expense of the gift.

Summary Points

Puja provides a model for understanding your role as a guest, and the dynamics of exchange and reciprocity that translate into expected behavior within business contexts. A positive, respectful attitude toward guests translates into India's open mindedness toward foreign companies, collaborators, and partners. What are the most important ideas to understand about puja that you can use to create strong business relationships?

> **Expect to be treated like an important guest.** Whether you are being introduced for the first time, or you are on your 10th meeting, any time you have contact, you are being invited into a

relationship. At first, this is not a relationship between equals. Guests are like gods and you have become a guest of the highest order, no matter the setting.

Learn to receive, graciously. Even though you are the guest of honor, do not let this go to your head. You are giving your associates the opportunity to fulfill their cultural obligations to make you comfortable, and practice humility toward others. Also forgo feeling any embarrassment or suspicion at the extent to which your associates may go out of their way to offer you something.

Be prepared to participate in a relationship of exchange. Up to this point, there is an accepted power imbalance at work. You have been welcomed and offered comforts and often even the topics of conversation revolve around you. The attention is unidirectional. Once you have accepted the hospitality offered, however, new expectations are created and a shift begins to occur. You have not only accepted food or drink, but also the possibility of further exchange with your associates based on the capital of satisfaction.

Expect to give something in return. It is now your turn to affirm your intentions to participate in this relationship, and complete the cycle of giving and receiving. In a healthy relationship, there will actually be many rounds, and by giving appropriate gifts, you will have not only completed a round, but begun another one. You are now inducted into a cycle of giving that mirrors the vitality, at any given point, between associates, and can be used to repair strained relationships as well.

Chapter 4

Ingredient 2: Role Expectations

Ashok, a senior brand and marketing manager, creates a marketing strategy for a new household cleaning product to be launched to young, urban women who maintain households and hold professional jobs. After analyzing current items being sold, the research and development team produces a prototype. When the prototype is market tested with a series of focus groups, Ashok's analysis finds it is missing the mark and fails to capture the attention of the intended audience.

Ashok immediately inquires into a delay for the product launch, communicating with his seniors to set new requirements and timelines that are then forwarded to his primary teams—product development, marketing, and channel. Using the feedback, he works with the product development team to change the objectionable features, notably the fragrance. At the same time, he delegates the marketing team to adjust the strategy to introduce new wording and imagery that highlight the time-saving features that received favorable responses. They also inquire into advertising in a new online magazine for women and TV ads in connection with an evening serial mentioned repeatedly in the focus groups. The channel team connects with a new distributor whose types of products and online accessibility match with the target audience. In addition, Ashok keeps an eye on how the new product aligns with other current products the company offers and whether it meets the standards of the overall environmentally friendly mission of the company. All three teams come together to create the improved product and marketing strategy under Ashok's adept management, ultimately leading to a successful launch.

Everyone has an official job description that lists the tasks and expectations of one's position. Getting hired relies on how well your employers think you will be able to complete these tasks successfully. Your qualifications become predictors of your potential to meet expectations. In order for Ashok to carry out his job of building and reinforcing overall brand equity for his company, his duties include a wide range of managerial responsibilities and roles. He must be a good communicator, an accurate interpreter of research analysis and metrics, a creative planner and integrator of online and off-line advertising strategies, and a leader with skills of delegation and decision making to be able to coordinate cross-functional teamwork. Each of these roles takes priority at different points over the course of a product pipeline, even though all are necessary to successfully complete the job. In addition, these different roles must also be coordinated to any higher principles to which the company adheres. For Ashok, this larger mission is one of environmental responsibility.

This idea of multiple responsibilities associated with a particular job, all of which are oriented toward a larger company mission, finds resonance across the globe. At the same time, this understanding of work finds cultural resonance in India with the particular idea of dharma.

Dharma, or duty, is a pervasive concept in India that sanctions a set of expected actions associated with each role one plays in Indian society. An individual's dharma involves multiple coexisting job descriptions based on gender, age, class, family relationships, and vocation. One can be a daughter, parent, wife, and manager all at the same time, each role requiring different actions at different times. Within business contexts in India, the concept of dharma explains two interrelated components to how people perform the roles expected of them in their job descriptions—the **dharma of individual roles** and the **dharma of mission.** The first involves the individual responsibilities assigned to each specific role, which constantly shift according to context and need. The second involves the coordination of these roles in alignment with a higher sense of what is the ethically right action and mission of a company. In this chapter, these two aspects of dharma present an important model for identifying and negotiating the roles and accompanying behaviors and expectations of your business associates. You will also be able to determine what is expected of you, based on which role you are playing at a given time.

Individual Roles

Dharma, at a root level, means "to uphold" or "to sustain." As a job description, when people do perform the dharma allotted to them through the roles they are born into and assigned, society is supported and stabilized. Whether a dutiful son who takes care of his ailing parents, or a teacher whose charge is to educate, each role has its place in creating respectful relationships and social contributions. While in modern India, some of these roles are undergoing revision, especially in the spheres of gender, the active pursuit of completing one's many roles to the best of one's ability is an inalienable right. Dharma continues to maintain its classification as one of the four primary aims of human life, alongside pursuits of pleasure, wealth, and spiritual attainments.

If dharma were just a human job description, people might feel free to ignore their dharma or not adhere to it. Dharma, however, carries a much stronger urgency rooted in the gods and heroes of sacred mythology that makes its fulfillment even more incumbent on every day people in Indian society. Different gods have very particular job descriptions and are expected to help out with different types of problems or situations in people's lives—a divine division of labor. Ganesh, the elephant-headed god, removes obstacles, while the goddess Lakshmi invites wealth and abundance.

In business, a division of labor also distinguishes between different roles and corresponding duties. Sunita, for example, works for a multinational American corporation as a call center customer service representative. Besides adopting an American name, Sheela, she also learns an American accent and stays up to date with sports trivia and the latest Hollywood basics as duties that help her create a friendly interchange and put her customers at ease as she is charged with solving problems with product quality, delivery, and billing. Milind, on the other hand, has a different set of duties as a floor supervisor in a business processing partner firm (BPO) for a European corporation dealing in financial services. The 25 associates working under him process loan and mortgage applications and have no need to learn these aspects of customer service as they interface only with the bank officers. Because of the odd hours that are worked to match business hours in Europe, Milind's duties include handling issues of absenteeism, keeping his workers alert and vigilant, and maintaining a strict vigil on the integrity of customer and company data to prevent possible misuse. A major crisis is averted during a routine check-up when Milind stumbles upon a file that had hyperlinks to very sensitive customer confidential data, including social security numbers and dates of birth that could be misused for identity theft. It is his duty to remedy this technical glitch by first alerting his bosses in India and Europe and working with a troubleshooting team until the data is protected.

Sunita and Milind may be just doing their jobs well according to an American model, but they interpret their own actions as their individual dharma in the workplace.[1] Dharma involves a larger set of dispositions that shapes behavior associated with the dharma of their different roles—from small courtesies to types of knowledge and actions performed.

Role Conflict

In business contexts, the different roles a person negotiates within a job and her respective duties also may come into conflict at times. A decision has to be made as to which role is more important at a given time to complete the overall tasks of a position. This conflict is expected to occur as part of the mindset of the Indian context.

One of the most well-known resources that exemplifies the powerful force of role expectations and conflict between roles in Indian society is found in the narrative of the god Rama. As a human incarnation of Vishnu, Rama's dharma is to incarnate into the world whenever chaos ensues in order to bring balance back to the world again. Rama ultimately succeeds in the task of dispatching the evil demon at the root of the chaos, and in the process helps many other characters through his salvific actions—as recorded in the beloved Indian epic, the *Ramayana*. The dharma, or duties, of Rama, as well as other characters in the epic, become a model of not only how to carry out one's duties in life, but also how to negotiate what action to take when different roles cause a temporary clash in expectations.

For example, in the beginning of the epic, Rama is faced with a conflict in the different expectations required of him from different roles in his life. He is the crown prince on the verge of being coronated as the rightful heir to the kingdom, and yet his stepmother has called on the king to make good on a promise he made years before to grant her any two requests as a reward for saving his life on the battlefield. Desiring to have her own son placed on the throne and Rama banished to the forest are the two requests that put the king into a moral bind—as he must carry through on his promise, even though he knows Rama is the rightful leader. Rama's responsibility as a dutiful son is to uphold his father's honor and promises, so he willingly goes into exile, instead of taking on the duties of being king. His wife, Sita, goes with him as her duty as his wife is to be by his side. In the forest, his wife is kidnapped by the evil demon, causing the pursuit of and ultimate demise of the evil demon that Rama had incarnated on earth to do away with originally. In the end, the conflict between dharma associated with different roles—crown prince, son, and husband, lead to the fulfillment of Rama's ultimate dharma as a god-hero.

In business and other contexts, the different roles of characters in the *Ramayana* may be appealed to as models to determine priorities and resolve the conflict between roles. The following example demonstrates how role conflicts may be negotiated, when a promise holds more weight than other factors:

> *A multinational company that sells and services office automation products uses local distributors to sell its products and services. A distributor violates the company's "no questions asked" policy of taking back defective products and refuses to entertain a return request of a local businessman for a very expensive color copier. Even though the businessman writes to the company and asks for help, his case gets lost in bureaucratic delays and he proceeds to utilize politicians and TV reporters to widely publicize his case. Nalini, a senior manager from the recently opened branch office in Bangalore drops her other projects and flies to Chennai to immediately assess the situation. She finds out that the distributor was at fault. With a priority on customer service, Nalini claims responsibility on behalf of the company and makes amends to the satisfaction of the aggrieved customer, including the offer of a discount, even though it was the distributor who was legally responsible according to contract obligations. Rather than distance the company from the public relations disaster, the senior manager invites the local businessman to appear in local advertisements and to endorse its products. He accepts and the company signs three new contracts within the month of the ad campaign.*

Nalini, as senior manager, has been charged to "fix the problem." To do so, she must negotiate and prioritize between different duties that come into conflict in this context. For example, she must uphold the ideals of the company, including the policies and promise of excellent customer service, as well as create profits for the company. She places customer service first when she agrees to take the short-term financial loss of the returned copier as well as offer a wholesale discount for future purchases in exchange for repairing and renewing the trust of the client. This decision results in long-term profit potential by turning the bad publicity into a marketing advantage that produces strengthened contracts and new clients. The well-managed negotiation of conflict between roles often leads to the most successful outcomes for all involved.

Dharma of Mission

Dharma contains a higher sense of duty or mission that has an effect on the behavior of each individual, as well as the corporation. In terms of individuals, you may encounter people whose behavior goes above and beyond their normative job description in their interactions with you as part of their understanding of dharma. For example,

> *Gordon, interactive marketing and e-commerce manager at a global beverage company in Atlanta, gets assigned to lead a digital marketing project in Mumbai, India. He has never traveled to Asia and is unfamiliar with its corporate culture. However, his counterpart based in India, Abhay, helps him in everything from work issues, such as making calls to colleagues to provide introductions and ease the way through the hierarchal networks in the India-based headquarters, to running errands outside of work that include finding appropriate clothing to attend an Indian wedding and finding an afterhours dentist when Gordon's tooth chipped. With excellent support in place, they complete the project before the deadline, but Gordon can't help but wonder about Abhay's behavior, and eventually mentions this to him. To his surprise, Abhay explains that he is only doing his dharma as a host to his business associate guest, and as a manager responsible for the overall productivity of every participant. Helping Gordon negotiate systems at work, social events outside of work and aiding in his general comfort level are duties that would be expected of him, and ultimately contribute to a productive environment for the project.*

Dharma not only applies to the different roles of an individual, but also is written into the mission statements and business plans of corporations in India. For example, Zeus Air Services, a freight forwarding service in India with both Indian and international clients, has this statement as part of their corporate philosophy:

Business with Ethics: Dharma, Artha, Kama, and Moksha

> Vedas acknowledge the existence of desire (Kama) and the pursuit of Wealth (Artha) to satisfy it but within the gambit of Social Responsibility (Dharma) for the ultimate Inner Satisfaction

(Moksha). It is this ethos which has inspired Deepak and Bharat Thakkar, founders of Zeus; not because of economic need but the spirit of entrepreneurship which runs in the Thakkar family... The main reason for this growth is "Care and Concern" for the Customers both "Internal" and "External." In this highly competitive and totally service oriented trade, team performance is the ultimate test. To that goal, each individual's needs and potential are assessed and then they are moulded together according to their strengths and weaknesses to ensure performance at the desired levels in Unison and Harmony under Inspirational Leadership [*sic*].[2]

In this excerpt, the mission of the company is founded on the four aims of life, including defining dharma as "social responsibility." The focus on team performance to create the highest customer service possible, uniquely tailored to each client, highlights a clear mission of dharma, based on these aims, to guide the entire company. This is an important framework within which many companies situate their endeavors in the business world.

The Indian corporation or business also envisions itself as having a particular role in the larger society in relation to other businesses, industries, government, or other organizations. Whatever role is designated to the company will be accompanied by expectations that will be carried out in their interactions and policies with others. This sense of mission or duty again has a stronger weight because of the religious and cultural background of dharma.

The subprime mortgage crisis that hit the American market in fall 2008 is a crucial example of the consequences of dharma failure by several players at many points. In particular, the hefty bonuses paid out to the executives of the investment banks and insurance companies from the government bailout money could be viewed as a senseless defiance of the dharma principle. Gurucharan Das, in his article, "The Dharma of Capitalism," disagrees with this last point as he adds that bonuses are part of contract obligations within certain corporations. Instead, he approaches this economic disaster through considering capitalism to be part of the larger mission. From this perspective, Das states that competition fostered by a free market system benefits many people, as long as it is a healthy competition and has the proper balance of regulations.[3] In order to pursue capitalism well, the individual roles people play must still be ethically framed, otherwise the mission, including capitalism, fails. In addition to Das's viewpoint, another response to the widespread market failure occurred in January 2008 when the Dow Jones created Dharma Indexes—the world's very first indexes that aim to track the financial performance of companies all over the world that conform to dharmic principles.[4] The interpretation of dharma in both of these responses points to a creative, yet practical application of the dharma of mission.

More often than not, corporate dharma often dictates decisions that put people or principles first, over profit at times. Starbucks' implementation of health care benefits for its part-time workers is one such example, costing the company profits in the short-term in exchange for long-term savings in terms of worker satisfaction, less turnover, and reputation. It means "doing the right thing," such as implementing environmentally safe products, or when conflict happens, to take the necessary steps to correct the situation. When seven people died in the Chicago area after taking Tylenol capsules in October 1982, the parent company Johnson & Johnson immediately alerted hospitals and distributors and halted Tylenol production and advertising. It ordered a nationwide recall of Tylenol products worth over US$100 million and ran ads and PR campaigns in the media advising people not to consume any products that contained Tylenol. Though such action brought Tylenol's market share from 35 percent to less than 10 percent, Johnson & Johnson handled the incident well and was able to rebound quickly.[5] What the company did is an example of abiding by the dharma that in the corporate situation would equate to corporate responsibility of being ethical and truthful to its customers.

Identifying Your Dharma

When you enter into business contexts in India, it is important to become aware of how you fit into both the **dharma of individual roles** and the **dharma of mission.** After identifying the roles of the people you are working with, and the extent of the duties associated with those roles, the most important task is to reconcile your own understanding of what roles you play in the American context, with the roles that are assigned to you by your Indian business partners and team members.

First, you may be assigned multiple roles. You will be able to distinguish these roles by interpreting what people ask you to do, as well as clarifying with your liaison. Second, once you have a sense about the range of roles, and corresponding duties, you will be able to determine what role is more important in a given context. The concept of dharma provides a model for knowing how to negotiate between the conflicting expectations of different roles. As long as the roles are clearly defined, expectations can be determined.

A corresponding task is to look at the wider picture. Can you identify the dharma of the company you are working with? If you are an American company utilizing Indian resources, how are your Indian partners defining their roles and responsibilities within your organization? Have you been clear about what is expected of them? Does it match their dharma? Taking the time to answer these questions can prevent larger problems from developing, especially if the goals are not aligned and need to be shifted. Similarly, appealing to the larger mission of the company as part of your strategy often meets with a more positive reception, especially if you are troubleshooting or asking for changes to be made. Understanding the dharma of mission in interaction with your own individual dharma creates clarity, respect, and alignment of purpose that benefits everyone involved.

Summary Points

Roles carry specific duties. Because of the way dharma permeates society, people tend to have a good sense of what their duties are, and are able to multitask the different responsibilities of these roles. However, don't expect people to take on roles that do not belong to them. Don't expect a manager to assume responsibilities outside of his or her role.

A clash in expectations is expected. Once you sort out the roles that belong to those expectations and what role is more important, the conflict can be resolved. The way dharma works provides an internal method of conflict resolution. For example, workers in an office may be disgruntled at a CEO who refuses to provide health care or a fair leave policy, because the dharma of a superior is to treat his workers "like a son or daughter." Superiors ought to look out for the well-being of the people in their organization or firm, and in return are given loyalty and respect. If a worker is late and leaves early, and does not complete his or her work properly, this is a problem of respect.

Know the dharma of the individual, as well as of the larger organization. Identify or clarify the dharma not only of each individual, but also of the company or partnership itself. These two aspects of dharma interact to produce behavior that often exceeds expectations.

Know your own dharma. What role do you play in your interactions with your Indian business associates? What role(s) have been assigned to you by your Indian associates? Do these two perceptions line up? If you can align or clearly define what role you are playing, you and your associates will know exactly what your expectations will entail. This allows people to interact with you in a way that can meet your needs faster.

Chapter 5

Ingredient 3: Business Caste or Hierarchy

A San Francisco–based Database Company wins a contract to install an enterprise resource planning (ERP) system for a multinational company's Indian subsidiary dealing in consumer products in Bangalore. The main application shells and modules have already been designed and developed when Brian, the project manager, and his team arrive in India. Their task is to install, implement, and test those modules with the company data, as well as train company executives how to use the applications. During the first meeting, the CEO, Krishnamurthy Subramanyam, presents the details of the project to his senior executives. Though attentive, Brian struggles to follow the presentation due to the accent and some of the word pronunciations. Interrupting the CEO several times, he asks "Krish" to clarify his doubts and repeat information. The CEO complies, although other executives in the meeting note Brian's informality and wonder why Brian appears to not be familiar with the project he is going to implement. The CEO assigns a senior executive, General Manager of Marketing, Mr. Dutta, to serve as liaison and oversee the project with Brian.

Over the next week, Brian and his team complete the testing and are ready to work with actual company data, starting with the payroll system. Mr. Dutta is away on urgent business, and instead of waiting until he is available, Brian goes to the Human Resources Manager to solicit the data. The manager defers and tells Brian to talk to his boss, the General Manager, Mr. Rao. He is in a meeting, so Brian goes to the Finance Manager, who also excuses himself and suggests that he makes an appointment with his boss. Brian feels frustrated with the situation but has no way of knowing that the mid-level managers do not have access to payroll data, only the general mangers have access to those files. After shuttling from one person to another, Brian barges into "Krish's" office. The CEO is on the phone with his secretary and a couple of people are waiting for him in the conference room for a scheduled meeting, however, Mr. Subramanyam listens and assures him that Mr. Dutta will return tomorrow. The next day Mr. Dutta supplies the necessary data while Brian openly criticizes the lack of cooperation of the managers and flow of information in the office that has delayed the project.

What Brian has just encountered is something called the "Indian business caste system," an internal form of hierarchy governed by age, seniority/rank, and gender, among other factors. That might sound like an oxymoron, given that social understandings of caste are usually considered to be traditional, family and community based forms of hierarchy, and business is conducted in the public world. However, Brian's frustrated attempts to access information without regard to the rules of this system, among other missteps, could have been avoided through having a better sense of the workings of power dynamics in the Indian context.

One of the most important aspects of doing business in India is learning how to navigate this system of hierarchy. Caste, in its original context, arranges society according to the family of birth, as well as occupation. In the past, the system enforced rules of social interaction between higher and lower caste members and structured a division of labor. It was one of the many factors leading to the oppression of those who fell at the lower spectrum or literally outside of the system as "outcastes." In modern-day India, discrimination on the basis of caste is illegal; however, the concept of hierarchy and division of labor still informs specific contexts, including places of work. In the above case example, Brian annoys his clients and becomes aggravated due to not being aware of how each company creates its own internal "business caste system."

This chapter identifies the major structure of the Indian business caste system, not as a literal "caste" identity, but as a way of interpreting some of the major features of hierarchy and power structures. The focus will be on suggestions as to how to work within this hierarchy to get things done. Misinterpretations of the hierarchy lead to violations of authority, slow down productivity and cause needless frustrations for people who do not know how to locate the right people with the pertinent information or skills. In Indian business, hierarchy is not just an administrative convenience; it is a mindset that regulates many aspects of behavior.

Origins of Hierarchy

The origins of the caste system are rooted in an early hymn found within the Hindu sacred scriptures of the *Vedas*. In this hymn, the

Ingredient 3: Business Caste or Hierarchy

creation of the universe occurs through the parceling of a Cosmic Body into various elements—the sun comes from his eye, wind from his breath, and fire issues forth from his mouth. Human beings come from different parts of this body, according to their birth and occupation. The priests and religious specialists come from the head, the kings and warriors from the arms as the regulators and protectors of society, the merchants, farmers, and tradesmen from his legs as the economic base of society, and menial laborers and servants from the feet.[1]

The head, as the most pure and highest part of a person, represents people who are responsible for memorizing and teaching the scriptures as well as performing religious rituals that were important in ancient India. The servant class comes from the feet, which are considered the most impure part of the body. Touching another person with your feet or with your shoe is still considered extremely disrespectful. Priests are at the top of this hierarchy, while servants are at the bottom.

In a society where a son inherits his father's property and by default his profession, many occupation-based subdivisions of caste, or *jatis*, emerged, such as goldsmith, ironsmith, milkmen, oilmen, cobblers, and washermen. The practice of marriage along caste and professional lines further consolidated the social hierarchy. People born into the upper castes would not do many jobs such as deliver mail, drive a truck or wait tables even in dire circumstances, since that would go against the dignity and honor of their caste and family. The most polluting of jobs were reserved for those who fell outside of the caste system altogether due to their work in managing human waste, sanitation, or dead animal hides. As "Untouchables," their touch was contaminating and these outcastes were not allowed to enter temples, draw water from the community well, or participate in social activities with other members of society. Gandhi renamed these outcastes as *harijans*, or people of God, but the members of several of these communities prefer to call themselves collectively *dalits*, or the oppressed lot.

With the signing of the Indian Constitution of 1950, discrimination based on caste became illegal. To further reverse the negative effects of the caste system, in 1990 Prime Minister V. P. Singh implemented part of the recommendations of the Mandal Commission established in 1979. The report of the commission proposed an extended system of quotas, or reservations, to several more socially disadvantaged segments of society in areas such as government service positions and admission to higher education than was previously found under the constitution. This reservation system is somewhat akin to affirmative action policies in the United States passed under President Kennedy in 1961, although the total percentage of reservations in India is much higher. In 1990, it began at nearly a 50 percent quota, causing riots at first, and has risen since then.[2] There is no mandate for hiring in the private sector industries, however the effect of reservations in education has led to a more diverse demographic with the skills required for working in business.

In business contexts, you will find many people who come from the third caste of merchants and tradesmen, especially since their families may have been in business for several generations. However, you will also find people from other castes and other religions.[3] In general, occupation-based caste distinctions have lost their valance. A person born to a family of goldsmiths remains a member of this caste subdivision (*jati*), even though she may have earned a doctorate in engineering, practices law, or uses her MBA to work as a consultant in marketing. Although systemic change is slow, several important figures in Indian history have risen above their lower or outcaste status, including Dr. Ambedkar, a dalit who studied at Columbia University in New York, qualified as a lawyer in London, and became a principle author of the Indian Constitution.[4]

The four levels of the caste system help explain the divisions of labor, or structure of the business caste system. The equivalent of the highest caste would be CEOs, COOs, VPs, or any upper-level executives in terms of power, authority, and access to what is deemed the most valuable information. The second level involves different layers of management. At the top are the General Managers as the rulers of delegation. Under them are the various ranks of warriors, the managers and assistant managers who mobilize their armies toward the task at hand. Sales representatives, BPO workers, data analysts, and call center teams would be examples of the third, and largest working class in a company. And a fourth class consists of cleaners, errand runners, mail delivery, and kitchen staff. All of these different classifications of people are needed for the smooth operation of the company. While this is similar to how companies are set up around the world, the relationships between these classes and lines of expected behavior are more pronounced in the Indian business context.

Crossing the Lines of Power

In the history of India, the first and second castes have often found themselves in conflict over issues of power. The Brahmins represented religious power and the ruling caste and warriors represented secular, worldly power. The ruling families needed the Brahmins, however, to conduct religious rituals that assured victories in war, healthy children to continue the lineage, and the overall well-being of the kingdom. In return, Brahmins relied upon the rulers as patrons who built temples and commissioned the priests for rituals. Clearly developed lines of conduct were implemented to maintain each sphere of power in a relationship of mutual interdependence to each other.

In business, the executive and management levels need each other to carry out the mission of the company. However, sometimes managers find the administrative vision is out of touch or unrealistic with what is possible to implement on the management level. At the same time, managers make the company function and harness the workforce to carry out the higher goals of the company. In traditional American settings, these same dynamics feel familiar. However, the ability to work across these lines feels very different in India.

For example, in America, a manager often feels quite comfortable walking into her boss's office to share ideas and may even spend social time with the boss as "buddies." This will vary to different degrees depending on the culture of the company. In the American online shoe company, Zappos, the CEO works in a cubicle alongside his other managers and workers, rather than behind a door in a corner office with a view. Google, and many other American IT companies are known for their informal corporate culture, as noted in even the dress code of T-shirts and khakis or jeans.

In India, conduct between different business castes is more formal and rigid. People who are senior to you in the hierarchy are addressed as "sir" or "madam," rather than by first names or nicknames. Managers do not wander into their bosses' offices to discuss ideas without an appointment. Socializing is uncommon between different ranks, although it is common within the same caste. A leading cross-cultural business anthropologist, Geert Hofstede identifies the formality of power structures across the globe according to a Power Distance Index (PDI). This statistical tool measures the degree of expected equality or inequality between people in terms of power and wealth. According to this scale, India scores a 77 in comparison to the world average of 56.5, and a score of 40 for the United States.[5] As a country with one of the highest scores on this scale, India requires a significant adjustment in formality for those who want to interact successfully in its business environment.

Managers who cross the lines of power are seen to dilute the authority of the executive or CEO, especially if done in front of other subordinates. Brian, the project manager from our opening example, inadvertently violated the internal business caste structure from the moment he addressed the CEO informally as "Krish" rather than as "Sir." As a cultural norm, people in India generally call each other by their last names. First names are primarily used for friends, siblings, and children. A new development, influenced by increasing globalization and familiarity with American management practices, is for upper level executives to insist on being called by their first names; however, it is important not to assume this informality without being given permission.

Although well intentioned, Brian's interruptions of the CEO, even if he had addressed him correctly, are perceived as a further sign of disrespect. If Brian had questions, he needed to clear them with Mr. Dutta, the liaison, at a later time and within an appropriate context. In America, there is more room to question or even disagree with your boss. Open disagreement with your boss in front of subordinates, even if done with respect, would go against the norms of hierarchy in India. If people see you being informal and voicing dissent with your own boss, both you and your boss will lose respect for crossing these lines. If you do disagree, do it in private.

GPS: Locating the Right Person for the Job

An electronics trading company selling fax machines and printers through several offices across India is facing severe competition. The company's new business manager in Pune, Sunil Seth is working out his profit margins for a big tender and wants to come up with the lowest discounted bid he could afford that would give him a chance at winning the tender while also covering his margins. He calls up his marketing manager at the corporate office in Mumbai for help. The marketing manager advises him to work with the prices he has and that he himself does not know the actual cost prices of the products. The company's products are imported into India from the Singapore office and the cost price to the Indian outfit is a combination of base cost price and an amalgam of duties, freight charges, insurance costs, and so on. Only the General Manger of Marketing and the CEO know the actual cost prices. Eventually the General Manager comes to Sunil's rescue and gives him the prices to quote for the tender.

Because of the way hierarchy is arranged in India, restricted access to information, as Sunil experienced, is a primary means of maintaining authority and rank. In American settings, it would be assumed that every person involved in a product has access to all the information about the manufacturing, costs, and sales of that item. This was also a source of frustration for Brian, who assumed that all mid-level managers of the appropriate departments would know the payroll data and be in a position to pass that information along. In short, access to information travels a short vertical path and not a lateral one as is common in the United States and other Western countries. Information is a privilege reserved for the top layers of management.

It is an embarrassment for a team member to be asked for information that is the purview of the supervisor, and the same is true between other ranks. Even if someone knows the answer, often times they will defer if the information is not part of their designated job. This may seem counterproductive, but there are many instances in which clear designations of workers' roles and tasks lead to efficiency.

Having an awareness of this system and not trying to work against it is the most important starting point. It is helpful to perceive the Indian branch or office as a family, with members that all have designated roles and responsibilities that contribute to the smooth operation of the whole. You will often be assigned an assistant while you are in India who can be relied upon to help navigate this system. If one has not been assigned to you, ask for one. Thinking along vertical, rather than lateral lines also will help you ask the questions to the right people and preserve authority and respect for the different layers in the company. It will also help you to create team confidence by not putting team members in the awkward position of not being able to answer questions that are not part of their rank.

Endogamy and Commensality: With Whom Do You Do Business?

In the social caste system, the upper castes developed strict rules in order to maintain boundaries between castes based on a spectrum of ritual purity and pollution. The highest caste was considered more pure. Their innate purity, according to this system, was necessary to sustain since it was their responsibility to memorize, teach, and perform the rituals associated with the holiest of scriptures. In order to enforce this purity, rules formed around situations in which purity could be violated, such as who you eat with and who you marry.

While rules have relaxed about who you eat with, it would still be considered rude to eat off of a common plate or to offer leftovers off of your plate to anyone else at the table. Shared appetizers (dips, bowls of peanuts, etc.), unless they can be divided and placed on each person's individual plate, should be avoided.

For many, caste is still an important factor in whom to marry, although this notion is changing rapidly as the young upwardly mobile workforce begin making their own marriage arrangements across caste and religious lines. In business, people do not restrict whom they do business with according to caste lines. However, because caste and community networks are predominant among people's social networks, these same networks in turn are invoked to find jobs, resources, and so on. People do business with whom they know, as they can easily get references from this caste network, and may even be distantly related to many of people they hire. This happens in other countries to different degrees, but because of the networks created by the caste system, this phenomenon can be more prevalent. In the Indian worldview, this leads to a stronger, cohesive company, in which mutual ties carry obligations and leads to forms of compliance transferred into the business context. This might appear like, and indeed at times may result in, some caste nepotism.

Your Place in the Indian Business Caste System

> *The multinational company in which Brian was struggling to complete his assignment also has outgrown being able to process customer service through a PBX system. To handle the growing customer base, the company hires a Hyderabad-based IT customer service company to implement a services automation project. From the beginning, Mai Sue, the project manager, models a very different approach. During the project presentation, she takes diligent notes and asks for a copy of the presentation from the assigned liaison to review anything she did not understand. Mai Sue and her team make an appointment and take the liaison, Ms. Awasthi, to lunch to further understand the project in its details and the expectations of the company.*
>
> *Whenever Ms. Awasthi is out of town and Mai Sue needs information, instead of going around the office, she contacts Mr. Awasthi's*

assistant to convey the issue to her directly. Mai Sue made sure in her message to note that she did not wish to disturb the CEO who also had that information. With respect to the care Mai Sue took to preserve the lines of authority, Ms. Awasthi made it possible to access the information remotely before she returned, so that Mai Sue could continue her work. The CEO often inquires in person as to whether Mai Sue has everything she needs. Mai Sue replies positively, but reserves any serious inquiries for her liaison.

Whenever entering into a new position or role in India, it is important to identify and mind the hierarchy. The liaison is there to help you negotiate that hierarchy and should be treated with deference unless invited to interact more casually. The caveat to this starting point is that as a foreign associate representing an American company, no matter your title, you will often be treated as higher in the hierarchy than you would normally place yourself. If you think you have identified your position equivalent in the office in India, you may be surprised at how that person treats you. The person assigned to help you is often of higher rank than you, sometimes having more education and experience. And yet, they may defer to you out of a respect for you as a "guest" (see ingredient 1), but also because you represent the higher status or interests of the foreign partner. As a result, the CEO may be available to you at any point during your visit, while your associate and team members will not have the same access. Your place in the hierarchy may be more fluid in practice, but it is important not to assume until you know that particular company's hierarchy better.

Summary Points

The concept of caste informs business as a system of hierarchy. Through having an awareness of the culturally specific manifestations of hierarchy, within which relations are informed or organized like a caste system, you will better understand the behavior of your associates in India toward each other, as well as toward you. There will be fewer missteps and inadvertent boundary crossings, as well as fewer frustrations as you are able to locate the right person for the right information. Everyone has their place in the system, and the sooner you learn to navigate the rank and distribution of responsibilities and information, the easier it will be for you to accomplish successful outcomes.

- **Caste is a mindset.** Hierarchy is pervasive to different degrees in different cultures. In India, the system of hierarchy is not merely an administrative convenience. It creates formality and gestures of respect that you will experience by both those who are higher and lower in rank to you.
- **Mind the lines of power.** Your boss is not your buddy in India. Err on the side of formality with people of higher rank than you, and if you disagree, do it in private to preserve the authority of you and your higher-ranked colleagues, supervisors, and bosses.
- **Think vertically, not laterally.** Information in Indian business moves vertically and access is granted to a select few based on rank rather than requirements. Identify the right person for the right level of information and don't expect everyone in the company to have equal access to information. If in doubt, rely on the person assigned to you to be your guide and identify the right person.
- **Congratulations! You've been promoted (temporarily).** Be prepared to spend more of your time with those of higher rank. You will be placed in a higher class during your visit to India, but this doesn't mean you are their equal or should be more informal. Respect and reciprocity should be the cornerstones of your behavior.

Chapter 6

Ingredient 4: Project Process and Management

Rahul works as a general manager of marketing for a Japanese consumer products company in India. In scanning the existing business environment in his industry, an American multinational company claims 70 percent market share, another Japanese company sits at 15 percent, and several other players have single-digit shares. The market leader holds an extensive network of offices and distributors across the country, a reputation for excellent customer service, high brand visibility and recall, a highly trained sales force, and an in-house manufacturing facility for select products. Rahul's task is to create and lead projects that will help his company claim a higher market share.

Several ideas float across his desk and are raised in various brainstorming sessions with team members. Since entering the market in India six months ago, Rahul's company has already established eight sales offices. But to match the competition's footprint, his company would require several more offices, a large number of sales representatives, more financial resources, and time. Rahul knows that a smart alternative is available in telemarketing. One particular project rises to the top of the list that would involve establishing a companywide telemarketing network. But where to begin? How does Rahul proceed to shape and manage a project to produce the best possible outcomes?

Each project a company chooses to develop and implement consists of several important steps. The early conception of an idea in the brainstorming stage, the choices in course of action and participation of specific people, and the completion of the assignment and a return to other aspects of work are all part of a journey that each project follows. In India, the process of the life of a project is similar to the steps of a pilgrimage, a pervasive practice undertaken across the religious landscape of India.

Pilgrimage, as a journey to a site of religious power, is not unique to India or its religious traditions. There are particular places for many religions in which the sacred has appeared in a specific form or for a delineated period of time, and that hold special blessings and benefits for those who make the effort to travel to see them. While each pilgrimage has its own unique aspects, in general pilgrimages follow a common outline of steps. The completion of each of these steps is important to the overall outcome of the pilgrimage and none should be skipped. Even though not inclusive to India, pilgrimage is a highly recognizable cultural feature within the Indian mindset and may be useful in certain contexts.

By using pilgrimage as a template, a manager gains a checklist that helps her to systematically prepare for the project, harness positive community-building features, and learn how to redistribute what is learned and accomplished into other projects. At the same time, missed steps can be avoided, and difficulties encountered on the journey can be turned into positives. Utilizing the features of pilgrimage creates

Pilgrims climbing the steps up to the temple of the Hindu god Murugan in the South Indian town of Palani, having recently passed the rest stop pavilion. (Natalia Zubko)

a potential management tool that brings a heightened commitment from everyone involved.

Setting an Intent

Hindus, Muslims, Buddhists, Jains, Sikhs, and Christians all have options to participate in practices of pilgrimage in India. The reasons vary from petitioning a god for the health of a child, doing well on an exam, or getting a job, to remembering and reenacting a sacred event in the life of a religious figure. The reasons can be for the fulfillment of worldly desires, to accrue merit to obtain a better rebirth or help one's ancestors, or to focus attention on one's own spiritual journey.

Before a person decides to undertake a pilgrimage, the most important action they take is to identify why they are undertaking the pilgrimage and what they want the outcome to be. The more precise the intention, the more motivation one has to see the journey to completion. In some traditions, this stage involves taking a vow, which carries a great deal of weight in terms of a promise to God.

A project may not need the weight of a vow to propel and motivate the participants to stay focused. However, if we understand a vow as a form of intention, every project would benefit from a purposeful clarification of the exact reasons and goals of the project before it begins. An intention is akin to a mission statement for each project that should be in alignment with the larger mission of the company, but also in alignment with each participant involved. A manager who sets a clear intention that everyone is on board with—and takes the time to hammer out disagreements, creates a level of commitment to a project from its inception. This project "vow" also serves to realign a project if people lose motivation or tasks get too far off track.

> *Rahul's mission is to assist in the growth of the company and gain market share. He cannot fulfill that mission without a proper infrastructure in place to support the amount of growth the company hopes to attain. According to the preliminary projections, if technology is put to use on a larger scale, it not only supports sales teams by generating and qualifying additional sales leads, but can also potentially help to build a customer database that can be used for various marketing and sales promotions in the future. At the same time, a telemarketing network is not as expensive to set up and maintain as several new*

offices and personnel. The intention to establish a telemarketing network that will provide ongoing support, generate further customers, and keep costs manageable is in alignment with the larger mission of the company. Convinced that this is the best project to pursue and with a clear intention, Rahul puts his proposal with cost and timeline before the management and awaits approval.

Preparation

Many people undertake various degrees of purification and preparation before they set out on their journey. This pertains to preparing body and mind ahead of time to varying degrees. In some cases, a person may give up certain foods, alcohol, and tobacco or other polluting substances to clear the body, and may exchange their everyday wear with special clothes. In general there is a sorting process that happens, as a pilgrim decides what is unnecessary for the trip and must be left behind, as well as what is required to complete the journey successfully.

Preparation is one of the most important features of a project. It is important to take the time to think through every aspect of what the project entails so that you can decide what you will need to complete the assignment. Are there certain people with certain skills that you need on your team? Do you need to arrange meetings or order supplies? Do you need to put together a presentation? It is just as important to also determine what you don't need in order to save time and money. What is unnecessary and can be left aside for another project? Paring down to essentials will help you travel lightly and still have exactly what you need at your fingertips.

> *Rahul secures the authority to oversee the project and is granted a three-month timeline to get it up and running. There are two important elements in preparing a telemarketing network: a robust application software running on a reliable computing network and a team of skilled executives high on quality and performance parameters. Rahul discusses his project with the IT manager, brings him on board and requests quotes from vendors. Rahul next approaches HR and requests the department to scout for agencies that could provide experienced telemarketing executives. In this project, it is a very cost-efficient option to hire a lot of skilled people quickly. He then discusses his expectations for the project with his marketing team and designates his marketing manager to codevelop a customized training program with the sales managers. The development*

of this training program now, even while the software program is being developed and tested, will save time in the long run—once the executives are hired, they can go straight into the training program. The input of ideas from both sales and marketing team members leads to training sessions that cover roles and responsibilities, reporting of relationships, performance metrics, and even hands on simulation and shadowing of calls.

Journey

When a person sets out on a pilgrimage, they choose as individuals to leave the comforts of their home and the routine of everyday life. Sometimes they leave behind family to take the journey alone, or travel with a spouse or companion as they begin to walk, take a bus, board a train, or take a plane to their destination. As they leave behind most of their everyday relationships, the first important change that begins to happen is the building of a new family, or community of pilgrims. As individuals make their way, they begin to identify with others who also are on the same journey.

A feeling of *communitas*, or bonding created through shared experiences, develops among pilgrims.[1] Communitas is nurtured through participating in many of the mandatory or recommended steps that people strive to do in order to fully complete every aspect of the pilgrimage. This may include giving money to beggars, bathing in a certain body of water, lighting a lamp at a particular temple, or singing devotional songs. People often share food and conversation to pass long hours.

In many companies, each project will consist of a new configuration of people involved in completing the assignment. While there may be overlap with people you become accustomed to working with in different departments, there can be variations that from a managerial point of view would be helpful to acknowledge. This means the recognition of a new team associated with each project, identifying who may not know each other as well, and building in time to get to know each other—sharing a meal, arranging meetings, and delegating assignments in ways that keep all project participants in contact and relating in new ways to each other. Being on a project together often creates its own sense of bonding, however a management style that is mindful of the benefits a strong communitas brings to the project, and purposefully nurtures it, can lead to more successful project outcomes.

Over the entire process of putting all the preparatory pieces into place, Rahul is keenly aware of creating situations in which team members from different departments have opportunities to meet and interact. He is sure to include at least the point person from each department—IT, HR, sales, and marketing—in each meeting, as he finds this leads to creative problem-solving sessions and better communication. Some of these meetings are purposely held right before or after lunch, with incentives to share a meal together. Even if the conversation is not directly related to the details of the project, Rahul views this time as a helpful way of forging good relational skills between team members. Because of this cross-department interaction, the IT department suggested and worked in collaboration to include an online simulation component to the training program being developed by sales and marketing. HR also received valuable input during the process of hiring since there were multiple opportunities to get immediate feedback from their sales and marketing team members, and invited them to sit in on interviews.

By the end of the second month, the software is installed, hiring is complete, and training is in process. A couple of trial runs of the software and the efficacy of results vindicate the usefulness of the project. With several hundred phone calls a day to prospective customers, a target number of qualified leads are produced before a company sales representative is sent out to make in-person visits. The outcomes of this approach include perfectly matched products, reduced sales cycles, and satisfied customers.

If executed properly the project has the potential to reduce or eliminate altogether the disadvantage facing the company in having a much smaller sales team than the market leader. Higher per capita sales can boost the income and morale of the sales team and bring in higher profits and margins for the company. Days away from the launch of the advertising campaign, there is excitement all around for a project that has benefited from the contributions of all members—a true team effort.

A second component of the journey involves an awareness of pacing and variation in rhythms of rest and rigor. Throughout the journey there will be rest points, as people recharge with food and tea. One may sit and rest for a bit in the shade of a tree, or on longer journeys, may take a nap or sleep. Street vendors have developed in larger rest areas to cater to pilgrims in need of supplies. As one gets closer to their destination, people prepare for the ardors of the final approach. This often involves an increased degree of difficulty or sacrifice to gain the most merit. In some places this may require fasting, crawling through a cave, or climbing a mountain or stairs.

Ingredient 4: Project Process and Management   61

Achieving a balance between stages of rest and revaluation with stages of increased rigor and productivity often is an overlooked aspect of a project. The drive to complete all projects under tight deadlines means the notion of a "rest stop" usually never enters the overall plan, especially in the American context. In the bigger picture, there are important plateaus in the life of a project in which setting the work aside for a short period of time allows team members to come back to the project with fresh eyes and often new insights. In the long run, this creates a stronger project, with fewer mistakes, and even saves time. A rest stop can take many forms, from short tea breaks to changing to another assignment for the day. A management style that acknowledges the value of rest stops and plans for them, especially just before particularly intense periods for the project, will be rewarded with higher quality of work and on-time assignments.

> *Rahul is satisfied with the project preparation. He convenes a meeting to thank all his colleagues and their teams, who were instrumental in making the pieces come together. Rahul institutes a two-day hiatus on the project, before the final three weeks of the project begin—a time to scrutinize each detail and push through any missing or delayed aspects. Over the two days, a barely audible phone conversation at home with a friend that cuts out repeatedly suddenly reminds Rahul of the poor telephone infrastructure in the country, a vital element in any telemarketing program. Though his company's branches have a sufficient number of phone lines to handle a peak number of calls during an advertising campaign, the vulnerabilities of the Indian phone network could disrupt the functionality of the project.*
>
> *On the following day, Rahul brings his concerns to his team and colleagues, including his boss. Discussions lead to a two-pronged strategy to address the problem. He puts his resources first at the temporary fix known as a "hunting line system" where only one phone number appears in an ad, but a received call hunts all available phone lines installed at the location and terminates the call at a line that is not currently being used. Several visits to the telephone office and some technical revamping produce the necessary adjustments. Two weeks later, this problem and all other details are worked out and Rahul's team successfully launches the national roll out of the telemarketing units. The risk of missed calls and thereby missed opportunities to generate potential sales leads is averted in time. A more permanent solution to the problem is implemented in the next upgrade through utilizing a*

national toll-free number, which is free of cost to the calling customers and follows a separate routing architecture capable of handling high business volumes.

Achieving the Goal: Not the End of the Journey

As a pilgrim encounters the sacred, participates in a moment of communion, has an audience with a religious teacher, or achieves other primary goals, the pilgrimage reaches its highest point of culmination. All the hard work has paid off and the pilgrim makes their petition and is grateful for the opportunity. An exchange occurs as offerings are made and blessings received. In most contexts, a pilgrim is given something to take back with them as a consecrated offering or special food, or a token to remember the moment.

While the primary goal of the pilgrimage, the reason for setting out on the journey to begin with, has been achieved, this is not the end of the pilgrimage. The return home includes important components, including taking the tangible blessings, often food items or other sacred substances, back home and distributing them to family members and friends. There is a process of reintegration back into one's ordinary life. In part this involves utilizing the new perspectives gained while on pilgrimage to transform one's everyday life. The entire process of a pilgrimage often reorients a person to what is important for them or helps a person participate actively in making changes in their life for themselves or their families.

When a project is completed, there is a range of responses, from a sense of accomplishment, or celebration to maybe even relief or reprieve if the project was intense. Following the pilgrimage model, the completion of a project is not the end in terms of what can be learned and reintegrated back into larger goals involving other projects and even the overall mission of the company. It is important to reflect on a series of questions: What was learned from the project? What can be carried forward that worked well? What did not work or what steps were missing that could be incorporated in the preparation of a project next time? Are there team-building strategies that could work in other contexts? Are there modules that could be transferred to other projects? Each project will be different, but has things to offer to other ongoing projects. This approach synthesizes resources and information in a way that leads to more cohesive overall management. It is a purposeful way of allowing the benefits of a project to infuse the entire organization.

Ingredient 4: Project Process and Management 63

Thanks in part to the success of the telemarketing project, the reputation of the company is being marked as technology savvy and customer-centric. But the most important contribution of the project is undoubtedly the substantial reduction in costs and expanded coverage of market. Pleased with increased productivity, Rahul proposes a similar kind of exercise built around the enhanced utility of cell phones to further reduce cost and motivate his sales team.

This is at a time (1998–1999) when cell phones are not common in India and calls are very expensive. Only a few companies provide cell phones to its sales people. Since Rahul's company already extends this facility to his sales team, Rahul proposes to tweak the reporting modality to the benefit of everyone. Normally sales teams show up at their respective offices between 9:00 and 9.30 A.M. "Work" starts with a few rounds of tea/coffee, smoking breaks, and small talk followed by a discussion of a "day plan" and itinerary (generated by telemarketing) between sales managers and sales representatives. Sales representatives then make phone calls to confirm their appointments before they leave the office. So, the earliest meeting a salesperson can attend is rarely before 11:00–11:30. At the rate of one hour per meeting (that includes driving time) a sales rep is able to call four to five customers at best in a day: one to two before lunch hour and two to three after lunch. At the end of the day, around 5:30–6:00, they come back to the office to report and go over their day-long activities. Sales managers generally stay and work in the office and only go on a call at the request of one of their reps.

Rahul finds the routine very inefficient. He proposes that sales reps need not come to the office in the morning at all. Instead they can go straight to meet the customer, which can be as early as 9:00–9:30 A.M. They report their activity to their sales managers at the end of the day when they can also finalize their day-plan and itinerary for the next day. Since they all carry cell phones, they can communicate back and forth to the office for information and support whenever needed. The new format enables a sales rep to comfortably call on seven to eight (instead of a maximum of four to five in the old format) customers a day and boosts call productivity by 40–50 percent. A higher number of customer calls is directly related to a higher number of sales orders, which brings in higher income for the rep and for the company. At Rahul's request a management meeting is called to make a decision to undertake a trial run of this new format at one location. After a three-month experimental run and favorable results, the new format is launched across the company. After a full year, the company records a 160 percent increase in sales productivity and a highly motivated workforce with rising income. The best part of the new format: it came absolutely free of cost. Rahul utilized the knowledge from the telemarketing project to creatively rearrange resources in an innovative way in another context.

Projects can be shaped in many ways, but all projects benefit from careful planning and attention to the different steps involved. Envisioning the project as a form of pilgrimage provides an important framework to work within the course of the assignment, whether one week or one year long. Pilgrimage reminds the project manger of the importance of maintaining a clear focus, prevents missing key components in the preparatory stages, utilizes team building to strengthen productivity, and gives space for the unexpected to be worked out. There is recognition of the lessons and benefits from one project being carried over to improve other projects, saving time and resources.

Summary Points

Know why you are taking the trip. As a manager, it is important for you to be clear on the goals of the project, and to be able to convey them to your team. Without this intention, team members may not be as willing to fully commit to achieving an outcome, especially if they don't know what is expected.

Preparation is essential to a successful project. Before you even make your first step, decide how best to approach the project, and what you will need at every stage along the way to best complete the assignment.

Community building strengthens commitment. Attention to communal interactions creates relational spaces for group ownership of the project to take place. Team members are more likely to give assistance to each other if managers foster inclusion.

Rest points are part of the journey. Building in moments in which the project can be set aside for a short period of time creates space for ideas for further improvements to surface. Much of the time when working on projects, we are so intensely focused on them we might miss the benefits of a fresh perspective that arise from the momentary, but intentional, change in focus.

Completing the project is not the end of the project. What lessons, resources, and knowledge you bring out of a project can be selectively carried forward to benefit other projects—why reinvent the wheel each time? Redistribution creates continuity.

Chapter 7

Ingredient 5: Leadership and Teamwork

As part of an ongoing nationalization policy dating back to 1969, the Government of India began to mandate all banks open one rural branch for every two licensed urban branches. Most banks wrote their rural branches off as a cost of doing business due to consistent losses. On the contrary, ICICI, a major Indian bank, identified the requirement as a new business opportunity. In 2003, ICICI launched the concept of rural lending through self-help groups (SHGs)—groups of 20 village women with little to no literacy, but who were more familiar with the customers in this market. After preparing the women through training programs and ongoing mentoring, the bank then lends to each SHG as a unit, which in turn provides loans to its members based on locally developed criteria. Empowered to self-manage, the SHGs prioritize, monitor, and collect dues with minimal interference from bank managers. Due to ICICI's groundbreaking Rural and Microfinance Solutions program, rural lending doubled in 2006 to reach $3.6 billion with over 3.2 million clients and an unbelievably high recovery rate of 98 percent. The program continues to affirm the knowledge and skills of its rural clientele as leaders and cocreate value through a growing network of partnerships linking SHGs to other community-based organizations and cooperatives.[1]

In the Indian context, the lines of power between leaders and team members are drawn in two directions. The prevalence of hierarchy is certainly felt in many organizations as supervisors draw strict lines of authority between themselves and their workers that dictate behavior of extreme deference. A tendency toward "deification" of larger-than-life leaders in politics and large corporations reinforces this power dynamic. However, there is also an opposing force to hierarchy found in Indian culture that does not completely erase these lines

Indian businesspeople working together as a team.

of authority, but demonstrates their flexibility. This integrative model recognizes leaders within the team in different capacities, rather than above them, as exemplified in ICICI's successful microfinance model that empowered leaders at the rural level. Depending on the context, either hierarchy or inclusivity can function as the dominant model of leadership at work. This chapter focuses on "the one and the many" as the basis for the integrative, inclusive model that redefines both leaders and team members and how they relate to each other.

Broader Cultural Contexts: Religion and Politics

The one and the many is a concept that pervades the Indian mindset. It identifies a particular integrated relationship between unity and plurality. Within the religions of the subcontinent, this idea is introduced in the ancient scriptures as a way to describe the relationship between the One Absolute and the multiplicity of gods: "Truth is One, the wise call it by many names" (*Rig Veda* 1.64.46). In the mystical Islamic traditions of Sufism, the chanting of the 99 names of Allah also underscores the multiple characteristics of one God. In both cases, each form or name encapsulates both a portion of and the entirety of that god at the same time.

In political arenas, "the one and the many" has become synonymous with "unity in diversity," a slightly clichéd motto that has met with different levels of success since the inception of the country. When India became a nation in 1947, it was founded on democratic, secular principles in an attempt to safeguard the diversity of the different regions and religious traditions that remained after the partition of the area into India and Pakistan. India became envisioned as a unity within which all the diverse parts were recognized not just as separate and crucial pieces of the whole; each part also represents all of India.

The concept of the one and the many also applies within business contexts. This chapter describes and prescribes a leadership style that approaches projects and the people involved in those projects as part of an integrated unity. One of the major benefits of this ideology is the ability to pursue a singular, unified vision—while *at the same time* envisioning each detail as being unique but all-encompassing parts of the whole. While this has repercussions at an HR level, it also can be a useful model for understanding, shaping, and creating cohesion in teams working toward a unified end goal. A leadership style that incorporates this vision has an advantage in utilizing a recognizable and respected approach to building the strongest team possible—a win-win situation for all involved.

The One: Leadership

In American contexts, the phrase "the one and the many" may bring to mind a division between two separate aspects: the "one," which stands separate from and perhaps above the crowd of others, or the "many." This is an interpretation of the role of a leader influenced by a competitive approach that values the drive toward individual achievement above collaborative efforts. Even the use of "and" has the potential of reinforcing this divide in spatial mindsets, as you have the "one" marked as here, *and* the "many" over there blending in and not standing out.

In Indian contexts, a very different interpretation is prevalent. The "and" actually denotes a coexistence between the one and the many that is integrated rather than divided. Leadership is defined by actions that facilitate the best collaborative work possible, rather than individual goals. Leaders recognize the value of each team member for their indispensible contributions to the whole, rather than as replaceable parts. One vivid example of acknowledging the value of each team member occurred at one of the leading information technology firms in India:

> *Infosys and its founder N. R. Narayana Murthy blazed a trail of unprecedented success that catapulted the company into becoming one of the most prestigious names in the IT industry. Murthy's visionary foresight, firm determination, hard work, and fair play helped him build a winning team of superlative performers and brilliant minds, who could service the most demanding of customers in the United States and Europe at a deeply discounted price but at world-class quality. His vision and principled leadership made Infosys a formidable player in the industry with an enviable A-list client roster that continues to bring huge profits year after year. In an unprecedented move, when the company went public, Narayana Murthy allocated the company shares generously to everyone who had participated in building the success and wealth of the company—including gardeners, office errand runners, and drivers. Each person, in proportion to their contributions, now had a financial stake in the ownership of the company, creating pride, respect, and a continued desire to contribute one's best to the team.*[2]

Acknowledging the value of every team member financially is only one possible marker of an integrative approach. The ability of a leader to foster investment and ownership in the fortunes of the company is the more important underlying task. In this second example, a company on the brink of failure was turned around due to creating a context in which employees increasingly took on more of the custody and control of the operations.

> *In 1989 a young Indian businessman named R. Jayakumar took over the operations of his family's 25-year-old flagship company Sai Petrochemical and Engineering Corporation (SPEC) that had diversified interests in fertilizers, pharmaceuticals, petrochemicals, and biotechnology. In the late 1980s, the Indian economy was running at a record deficit and inflation was high, leading to a slump in demand for many SPEC products coupled with a lack of credit options.*
>
> *Under tremendous pressure, Jayakumar called a meeting with not just his management team, but all employees, announcing that all ideas were welcome in working to resolve this SPEC family crisis. Employees and managers met in small groups to exchange their ideas. Two pragmatic options were to cut salaries, which would further hurt the*

employees since they were barely surviving in an inflated economy, or lay off employees, sacrificing some of the company's employees to save the rest. As a conflict with the employees' union would result from either option, in addition to morale loss to the company, the employees proposed a modified alternative. A salary cut would be accepted only in exchange for three things: an incentive plan giving the employees a substantial share in company profits, a 50 percent pay cut for Jayakumar and the management team, and complete transparency in financial transactions, marked by a member of the union cosigning every check the company wrote. After a proposal was created and strongly backed in collaboration with all ranks found within the company, it was accepted and implemented.

The results were transformative. Within six months, the company erased its losses and broke even. To save money, employees started handling most of the work the firm had contracted out to other companies and business partners. They served as security guards and cleaners and helped run the company cafeteria. The union official nominated to provide oversight scrutinized every expense. Through such dedication, SPEC made a small profit at the end of the year.

The successful turnaround of SPEC led to further decentralization of management and structure, along with an increase in freedom of information and diversified decision-making power. Employees set salaries and hours, and had access to profit margins and corporate secrets such as product design. Line workers and engineers decided how and when they would produce new products, and set prices. Multiranked committees of employees scouted for locations for new plants. The explosion of energy, enthusiasm, and flexibility discovered during the crisis ultimately created a corporation consisting of business partners with direct stakes in the fortunes of the company. Within three years, SPEC became one of the fastest-growing companies in India.

A moment of crisis often can be turned into a moment of opportunity, as evidenced here in this working model of SPEC, based on an amalgamation of several case studies. Leadership, for Jayakumar, involved a recognition of needing to enlist the problem-solving skills of a wider pool of employees by way of encouraging investment in the overall well-being of the company. This means a commitment to taking the suggestions of different levels of employees seriously, but also knowing where to draw lines and how to keep the larger goals of the company in mind or the larger vision. In this case, temporary financial benefits were sacrificed (salary cuts), along with certain aspects of control (union oversight on checks, etc.), allowing for a diversification of authority to occur. In the long-term, these sacrifices helped gain the trust of more employees, who felt their suggestions were being taken seriously, creating a willingness to pitch in even more in ways that would benefit the entire company. While an idealized model, aspects of inclusion may be an important strategy to enlist, with the appropriate forms of checks and balances that will look different in each context.

Infosys and SPEC demonstrate an inclusive model that recognizes and supports the creation of leadership qualities diversified within the team. There is still a leader, but that leader is defined through fostering leadership in others at the same time and creating the conditions under which that can happen. The one and the many coexist with the lines becoming purposefully blurry at times between the two categories.

The Many: Teamwork

As more leaders are created from within the team, there is less and less of a difference between the two categories. However, it is not just a permanent state of integration that does away with the distinctions completely. Rather it is a spectrum in which leaders often have to make the big decisions, but how they go about it depends on how well they see themselves as part of a team, rather than above it. On the spectrum of leadership and team membership, the mark of a good leader is to know where to be on the spectrum within a given situation, and to not remain stuck at any one point. When does one step back or step up? Knowing that this is fluid rather than fixed is integral to understanding or entering the model. The following example demonstrates this movement along the spectrum, at a moment when it tilts toward fostering teamwork.

> *Computer engineer Steve works for a Japanese consumer electronics company in California in its Display Products Group (TV, LCD, Monitors, etc.). After spending a year as a systems manager in Tokyo, he joins the management team in India as head of IT under Naveen Raje, the newly appointed President of India operations. Raje had started at a multinational company in Mumbai before earning his MBA from Wharton, spending 10 years consulting for Fortune 500 companies before returning to India to direct the finance division of a U.S., MNC. He became CFO in five years and was evaluating his options*

when the Japanese company selected him to lead and launch entry into the Indian market.

Under Raje, Steve and the rest of the core management team prepare for the first major challenge in setting up a viable sales and service network in a market that shows ample opportunities for growth, but is dominated by well-established multinational and local companies supported by excellent distribution and logistics capabilities. A corporate and marketing strategy must also be outlined, including sales projections and annual budget.

In the first meeting with his colleagues, Raje shares the projection brief from headquarters that is to take the company to a comfortable second position within three years and become the market leader in five years. He does not lay down any numbers or targets, but instead asks his regional business managers to study the research report, develop an aggressive but realistic sales plan, and assemble a sales and service team to achieve that within their own local markets. He commits senior management to work with the sales teams and extends full support. The group agrees on an eight-week window to develop the groundwork before reassembling. Raje reminds the team that nobody works "for" him but "with" him.

This bottom-up instead of conventional top-down approach to management takes everyone including Steve by surprise. Taking this model as a cue, the regional managers build each of their branch plans as the sum total of the delegated individual plans of each member of their sales team. When the regional business managers reassemble after eight weeks, Raje and the group recognize the unique contributions of each unit and begin the process of weaving a cohesive national plan that highlights these different strengths. The end result is a business plan that is 20 percent over the revenue target Raje's bosses had in mind, and creates a collective ownership of the plan, while fostering respect between the different branches. As a sign of cohesive teamwork, the group also proposes its own evaluation of branches based on per capita sales productivity, rather than units sold or revenue generated, signaling an internal respect that reinforces the equality of everyone's contribution. The launch is a success and the work of the team of regional branch managers sets a foundation for growth that takes the company to market leadership by the first quarter of the sixth year.

What Steve experiences under Raje's leadership over the six-month prelaunch period turns out to be a classic workshop in inclusive management that relies on the twin pillars of delegation and empowerment. Raje creates an environment in which leaders rise from within "the many" to codevelop a plan and set the parameters for responsibility over implementing, carrying out, and evaluating shared goals. This approach unleashes creativity, utilizes strengths and counters limitations, and often leads to higher than expected outcomes. The more Raje, as "the one" reinforces self-determined direction and behavior from within his teams, the more productivity occurs.

The One and the Many

Leaders and team members are redefined as part of one another. Teamwork happens through creating space for each member to be a leader. The "many" cannot become leaders without an initial leader who sets the foundation within which to bring out their unique contributions in a cohesive, rather than competitive way. This does not work if the "one" is too invested in their own position and power over others. The "one" who learns when to step in, and when to step back and delegate in a way that leads to empowerment, exemplifies the best of what the one and the many as an Indian model has to offer in terms of management styles. For example, Infosys has actively worked to create a viable model of "collective leadership" that exemplifies the one and the many.

In August 2006, at the age of 60, N. R. Narayana Murthy retired as the company's chief mentor and chairman of Infosys Technologies Ltd. In July 2009, another change of leadership took place as Nandan Nilkeni left to head the new government program that will issue high-tech IDs with biometric data in a microchip to over one billion Indians. These changes in succession are not disruptive due to an intentional grooming of leaders from within all sectors of the company that began back in 2001 with the founding of the Infosys Leadership Institute in Mysore. At that time, the company identified 400 leaders out of the nearly 60,000 employees from across the globe in keeping with the company's multinational, multicultural image on the basis of several performance-based parameters, including creativity, devotion to being ethical and sincere in dealings, and a commitment to strive relentlessly in pursuit of excellence. Each leader undergoes sustained training in a personal development program (PDP) to prepare its executives to handle the external and internal business environment and becomes adept at "thought leadership" in order to create better customer value.

Beyond the Institute, there is a three-tier mentoring process that allows leadership skills to trickle down into different team levels. Tier-1 of the Infosys Management Council, which consists of the company's board of directors, mentors Tier-2 leaders who in turn guide the Tier-3 group. This diffused model of leadership treats each of its employees as an integral and indispensable part of the company and allows them to move up in the management echelon based on their abilities and competencies. Leadership opportunities emerge within all levels. The effort to create a huge pool of leaders ensures smooth transition of authority, as witnessed in the rotation of roles even at the highest levels.[3]

The one and the many are coexisting principles that encourage collective leadership qualities. It is not a dynamic used in all situations or by all managers, but currently is showing up in businesses large and small as a viable alternative at the other end of the spectrum of hierarchy.

Summary Points

The one and the many are defined by integration, not separation. The gap between leaders and team members that is reinforced in a hierarchal model is more fluid from this perspective. Leaders and team members can only be defined in light of one another.

A team member is not a part, but is the whole. Each person is not just a partial contributor to the team or a particular project, but encompasses the process and goals of the entirety. This collective approach fosters joint ownership and investment in a project. Team investment leads to stronger commitment to a unified goal.

A leader is defined by the ability to foster leadership qualities in others. Leaders are necessary to the smooth operation of an organization. The best practices of leadership in this model promote initiation and collective management from within the group.

Chapter 8

Ingredient 6: Risk and Action

Michael works as Resource Planning Manager for a major telecommunications company in New Jersey. He is currently working in Hyderabad with an Indian IT company that manages his company's customer services and provides other logistical support. When he receives a proposal for a research and development (R&D) project for 3G services he finds himself in a thankless situation. Michael is very pleased with the quality of work and professionalism of his Indian colleagues. He is confident that the new project will meet or exceed his expectations and those of his bosses. R&D work in the United States has not been very satisfactory so far and has cost the company millions of dollars. Resources and personnel proposed for the new project look very impressive, both in terms of people with excellent qualifications and proven expertise in technologies and tools needed for the job. Locating an R&D project in India would also potentially result in a huge cost savings.

However, there is a downside to the project, as it will cut hundreds of jobs in the United States and will cause severe hardships to many of Michael's coworkers and friends. He is also aware that the competition has been investing heavily in R&D projects and many players are planning to launch several new services in the coming months. If his company lags behind in its R&D effort and slips on introducing newer services it will certainly witness a decline in its market share and profits, and eventually affect the long-term viability of the company. How does Michael decide what to do?

How do people make decisions? How does one weigh their options before making a choice? Before an action is taken, a person considers many factors specific to the particular situation, alongside more intangible dynamics arising out of a person's background, culture, personality, and habits. One of the most subtle, unstated and seemingly contradictory factors in decision making in Indian contexts is shaped by one of these cultural and religiously influenced intangibles—the ideal of *karma yoga*—defined as action without attachment to the outcomes.

In a target-bound, results driven business culture, karma yoga seems at odds with considerations of profit, a key outcome that guides overall decision making in all businesses. However, karma yoga bears a strong imprint in the decision-making process often at points of impasse as a way to frame risk. How can a person live up to the ideal of their responsibilities if they are too focused or stuck on future unknowns? Sometimes they must let go, temporarily, of the outcomes—rewards or failures—in order to leap. In these cases, profit, while a potential, but uncertain outcome, cannot be the first priority in triggering the action in the moment. Risk is guided by appropriate actions determined at the point of decision making based on principles of duty, rather than on future incentives. This chapter describes the characteristics of right action according to the principles of karma yoga as modeled in the *Bhagavad Gita* as a potential resource for understanding decision-making processes.[1]

The *Bhagavad Gita* is a short philosophical dialogue found in the middle of the great Indian epic, the *Mahabharata*. In this excerpt, the protagonist, Arjuna, finds himself at a moment in which a crucial decision must be made. He has to decide whether to engage in a battle in which his own family members may die in order to establish the rightful succession to the throne. At this moment of crisis, he puts down his weapons and refuses to fight. It is not until Krishna, a prominent Hindu god who is acting as Arjuna's charioteer, leads Arjuna through all the reasons as to why he must take a particular action and go into battle that he enters the field.

While those in the business world hopefully do not find themselves having to make decisions of such dire life and death consequences as Arjuna, there are weighty decisions having to be made on the battlefield of business every day. The advice that is proposed in the *Bhagavad Gita* has been considered so useful, it is regarded by many Hindus from the middle and upper classes as the "bible" for those in the midst of a dilemma, or having to make a decision, whether large or small. Even without the devotional message that resonates with many Hindus, there are important points that Krishna makes in his advice to Arjuna that can be helpful to decision makers in any context.

Principles of Karma Yoga

What part of Krishna's advice is useful for people today? What characteristics of karma yoga translate well as a model for making decisions? How does karma yoga explain how your business partners or team members may be making decisions in your next business meeting? How would Michael make his decision regarding outsourcing the R&D project if he was being guided by karma yoga?

There are six primary principles at work in the mind of a decision maker influenced by karma yoga. The best way to begin to see the principles that grow out of this idea is to analyze them in connection to a few narrative illustrations.

Story 1

> *Rohini Dua is Marketing Director for a Korean consumer durables company in India that sells appliances and electronic gadgets. Two years after entering the Indian market, Rohini hires a marketing company to help her develop better insight into her marketing strategy and fine-tune her product portfolio according to the buying behavior of her customers. The contract requires the marketing company to put 60 research associates to work at several locations of the company under the supervision of marketing manager, Sandeep Garg, who reports to Rohini. Sandeep would certify their work and submit their timesheets at the end of a two-week period to the HR & payroll department with a request to pay the marketing company, which would then release payment to the associates. Work starts and Rohini is excited about the project.*
>
> *All is well until a couple months later, when Sandeep notices a sizeable drop in productivity and morale. Upon investigation, he finds that the associates are not getting paid on time because HR & payroll delays payment to their company. Some employees have not received their checks for over three weeks. When Rohini learns about it, she deliberates on her duty and limitations. Since HR & the payroll department are bound by contract to release payment after satisfactory completion of services by the associates, she first brings the matter to the attention of her HR counterpart. She hopes for a quick resolution of the problem. However, when the problem persists after a lapse of another two weeks, she takes further action since the associates work for the marketing department. Their low morale and declining productivity is creating a negative impact on the quality of research and overall cost efficiency. She prioritizes the matter in the next management meeting. After apprising*

> her boss of the development and consequences, the matter gets urgent attention and a timely resolution amends the situation. Rohini's recognition of her responsibilities and persistent action ultimately leads to the launch of many new products targeted at consumers based on the findings of the project.

From the example of Rohini, we begin to understand two of the primary foundational principles from the perspective of karma yoga. As marketing director, Rohini has a fairly clear set of responsibilities, but when her contracted research associates end up with a payroll glitch that is having an effect on productivity, it becomes part of what she now needs to pay attention to. Once Rohini realizes that this is an issue that was up to her to problem solve, she had a choice to act or not act in the situation. According to karma yoga, inaction is not an option, and so Rohini persisted until she was able to resolve the payroll related issue for the employees. The first two principles exemplified in story 1 are summarized here.

Principle 1

Determine whether a particular situation is part of your responsibilities to do something about. Clarify who is in charge of the situation. **Determine your role and corresponding responsibilities,** and if the problem falls under your jurisdiction, it is time to step up and decide what to do. If it is not up to you, make sure the person determined to be in charge knows there is something that needs to be done.

Principle 2

According to karma yoga, if you have determined that a particular situation is your responsibility, **you must take action.** Inaction is not an option. To avoid action or cause unnecessary delays only prolongs problems.

Story 2

> *Srinath Shetty is General Manager for Corporate Strategy & Planning for an Asian office equipments company in Mumbai. While several rival companies have been selling their products in India for over a decade, his company delayed its market entry due to several restrictions and cumbersome legal requirements for foreign companies wanting to do business in India. Now, after they have launched their products and services in the country they are faced with a peculiar rival: their own*

products that sell in the black market and reach the country through gray channels. These are basically discarded products from the American and European markets, which are imported as junk, repaired, and resold at heavily discounted prices. The majority of these products are high-end and have a long product life cycle, which directly cannibalize sales of the company's genuine products in the market.

Srinath initiated legal actions against some of the companies involved in the racket, but his frustrations still run high since legal cases prolong for years and do nothing immediately to improve product sales and profits. He hits upon a creative solution, but before embarking upon his ambitious plan he presents his idea to his boss, the company president and the World HQ. After seeking their advice and incorporating a few of their suggestions, he unveils his plan of importing genuine refurbished products to compete with the challenges of the gray market. In North America and Europe environmental regulations require the original manufacturers to recycle working components and parts of their discarded products. Companies reuse these parts in the manufacturing of new products and sell them as "refurbished" products at discounted prices. This is better for the environment as well as serving price-conscious consumers in developing countries.

Many of the products selling in the Indian gray market are available as refurbished (RF) products in the company. Srinath develops a marketing plan to import and launch them in India. This is a risky move in that he is essentially flooding the market with cheaper versions of their own products. He carefully targets industrial and commercial customers who usually prefer authentic products and channels if prices are competitive, over the usual gray market operations. Within a year Srinath's strategy demonstrates a clear impact on the market and the gray market registers a significant decline in its market share. Srinath follows up with attractive offers to take back "unauthorized" products and exchange them with refurbished products supported by his company's guarantee and services. In a span of three years, Srinath's strategy results in close to 90 percent of the market being replaced by genuine products, an unexpected success he had no way of predicting when he first proposed his plan.

Srinath's plan to enter the grey market of refurbished products on the surface may have looked like a detriment to profit making through competition with the company's own authentic products. The risk involved in this plan was high, and only after seeking the advice of trusted mentors did he seriously pursue this line of action. As profit was not the immediate outcome, Srinath's focus needed to be on his duties to the company to creatively problem solve, without having a direct sense of what the outcomes would hold. If his plan had to be tied to a certain percentage of profit, an unknown factor in this case with great possibility for failure, there is a chance it would not have been implemented. The principles of karma yoga from story 2 can be summarized as follows.

Principle 3

Seek the advice of trusted advisors. If it were not for Krishna, Arjuna would have remained on the sidelines, refusing to participate or complete his duties. It is a time-honored tradition to search for the best advisors—usually seniors or elders—to hear their wisdom on the topic. Ultimately the decision rests on your shoulders, but there is respect for listening to the input of others.

Principle 4

Proceed without regard (be impartial) to failure or success. In short, this is what is meant by not having attachment to outcomes of any kind. As you work through your options, rethink those that depend on measuring up against certain markers or results. By basing decisions on future results or projections, it potentially limits the creativity of solving the problem in the present.

Story 3

Nitin Bapat and his wife Indira are successful biochemists in the United States with many patents to their credit. They decide to return to Mumbai with ambitious plans to start a biotechnology company in India. They choose India because it is one of the fastest growing economies in the world and is home to the largest pool of technically qualified graduates they would like to employ for their venture. Relaxing in the spacious bungalow of his parents in posh Malabar Hill, Nitin deliberates with Indira on the possible location choices for their business. They both grew up and worked in Mumbai before heading to the United States for their doctoral studies and have an extended network of friends and family in the city. Nitin's parents are reputed surgeons while Indira's father runs a thriving diamond business. But the high real estate prices in the city are a major concern for them. They know that the large number of graduates and technicians they plan to hire will not be able to afford decent housing in Mumbai and will have to commute for at least a couple of hours each way from the more affordable northern suburbs.

Nitin and Indira wish to create a caring company that fosters mutual respect and provides a good quality of life for the employees of the company. They also know that this will directly result in high work productivity and low employee turnover. With these goals in mind, the couple reaches the conclusion that intensely crowded and exorbitantly expensive Mumbai will not be the right choice for them. The search for an alternative location that can serve best the interests of the company as well as those of the employees finally ends at Pune. Only a 15-minute flight away from Mumbai, this city is far more affordable to employees the company plans to hire. Pune is a great educational hub and many technical and other institutions dot its landscape. Its international flavor, entertainment options, and a happening nightlife are added attractions. Nitin and Indira feel at peace with their decision. In the years that follow, the company makes a good name for itself not only for its products and inventions, but also for its management philosophy rooted in principles of the greatest good for the greatest numbers.

For the Bapats, many hard economics factor into their decision-making process based on profit and solvency, and yet at the same time, attention to quality of life for their employees leads to other benefits. The reputation of the company grows because of this commitment to their employees and a low turnover rate attracts higher quality employees. While both Nitin and Indira have important family ties to Mumbai and would like to be based there for personal reasons, it is ultimately in the greater interests of more people involved in the company to be based in Pune. Story 3 illustrates the final two primary principles of karma yoga as follows.

Principle 5

Give up individual rewards. Do not act with the assumption that you will gain something personally out of your actions. Ask yourself who would this action benefit? If it is an action that primarily benefits you only, demote the idea.

Principle 6

If the action benefits the greatest number of people, aligns with the roles of all team members and participants involved, and provides **service to the greater good,** more than likely it is the right action to take.

Philanthropy and Karma Yoga

Philanthropy is a natural extension of karma yoga. There are many examples in India of people who identify a cause as their responsibility, and decide to take action regardless of possible failure, personal hardships or promises of individual success. These pursuits often end up benefiting larger segments of society as a form of service. In working with a business plan, philanthropic aspects often are included from this desire to benefit underserved populations. The profit created from a viable business operation creates the possibility for free or low-cost products or services to be offered. One example that illustrates this approach is the founding of a comprehensive, low-cost eye care facility, known as Aravind Eye Hospital.

> *In 1976 Dr. G. Venkataswamy, an eminent eye surgeon, started a modest 30-bed hospital in Madurai with his retirement savings and some government financial help to provide quality eye care with a simple vision: eradicate needless blindness in his home state of Tamil Nadu. His business plan contained a philanthropic element—to serve moderately paying as well as free patients. He looked at high productivity and large volumes as prime factors to keep his business viable and generate a surplus to expand its services and add new locations.*
>
> *The group now has five Aravind Eye Hospitals (AEH) in the state with over 3,600 beds—nearly 80 percent for free patients. Starting with cataract surgery, it has now added several specialties and ancillary divisions: Aurolab, for manufacturing intraocular lenses; a training center named LAICO (Lions Aravind Institute of Community Ophthalmology); a research center for women and children named Aravind Centre for Women, Children and Community Health; and the Rotary Aravind International Eye Bank. All the activities of these divisions relate to the core mission of preventing or correcting unnecessary blindness.*
>
> *Despite a high majority of free patients, the Aravind Eye Care System has always been financially self-supporting and never depended on government grants except during government sponsored free eye camps. It built all its hospitals with the accumulated surplus. AEH's purchase of the best quality equipment and a top of the line IT system, while keeping rooms sparse and functional, indicate that the emphasis is placed on quality care for patients. They constantly work on developing sustainable systems that better utilize doctors and heighten their productivity in order to extend their services to as many people as possible.*[2]

Is Outsourcing in Alignment with the Principles of Karma Yoga?

In the beginning of the chapter, we started with the example of Michael, a Resource Planning Manager who was in the middle of deciding whether to outsource an R&D project to India. Utilizing the principles outlined above, he had already determined that this was his responsibility, and that it would be up to him to make the decision. If he was guided by karma yoga, the scenario might continue as follows:

> *For a couple of days Michael goes over the details of the proposal with his Indian colleagues. After careful deliberation, he contacts a few select mentors within the company in the United States and other branches for their advice. Michael worries about his U.S. colleagues and the disruption and hardship they will face. At the same time he sees how this project would place the company on the cutting edge of technology and innovation and win more market share. What this project potentially would lay the groundwork for is freeing up resources to create new job possibilities back in the United States eventually, but not without temporary losses first. It is ultimately his duty to utilize the resources of the company in the most efficient and productive way possible to continue growth in the long term. He decides to go ahead with the project, even though he may personally lose some friends in the process. His judgment call includes a short-term sacrifice for the benefit of the most people in the long run. A viable company with new products in the pipeline means more jobs and more stability to jobs in the bigger picture.*

The principles of karma yoga would support the outsourcing of the project in this scenario. However, each decision will have its own context within which the different factors must be weighed. In other cases, the sacrifice of too many local jobs would damage the reputation or the internal cohesiveness of the company too much. In that case it might be a better option to make other decisions. But if the decision maker is keeping in mind the principles of karma yoga, then the pursuit of actions that benefit the greatest number of people in the long run will always be at the forefront of the factors involved.

The Bottom Line on Karma Yoga

Karma yoga changes the very definition of success and presents its own risk strategy based on the right action, not predetermined goals.

Not every person in every situation works with the principles of karma yoga, but it is a prevalent ideal that works at the cultural level to influence decision making in many contexts you may encounter.

In karma yoga, the bottom line is not the most important factor in making a decision. At first, this may make karma yoga appear to be at odds with a business ethos that focuses mostly on profit margins. Instead, what happens is that through the principles of karma yoga, decisions that are pursued without individual interests in mind and align with the most people often will ultimately be financially viable and create greater rewards, financial and otherwise, in the long term.

Summary Points

If it is your responsibility, it is up to you to take action. When working with your Indian business partners, it may be a helpful strategy to frame requests as part of a person's responsibilities. If an action is determined to be part of a person's duty, an appeal can be made to take action.

Seek advice from trusted mentors. Respect toward elders and those of higher rank lends itself to soliciting solid counsel from those whom a person trusts before action is undertaken. Keeping these mentors in the loop also creates long-term support for ideas.

Be impartial to failure and success. At times, it is important to let go of future-oriented outcomes in order to focus on creative problem solving in the moment. This does not exclude the potential for success, but sometimes is a necessary move that frames more high-risk actions where the outcome is indeterminable.

Give up individual rewards in exchange for serving the greatest number of people. A helpful strategy is to ask who benefits in a particular situation. If a majority of the people involved would gain advantages, even with a potential or temporary loss to individual benefits, this factor may be what tips a colleague toward a more service-oriented decision.

Chapter 9

Ingredient 7: The Pursuit of Wealth

Outside some of the largest sari and jewelry houses in the market district of Chennai, workers construct multistory scaffolding made of roughshod branches, twine, and countless strings of electrical lights. On the first night of Diwali, a New Year festival of lights, the owners plug in the cords for the first time, illuminating complex animated designs. The most popular theme is a beautiful woman sitting or standing on a lotus, one hand raised in a blessing gesture, and another stretched out and spouting an animated waterfall of never-ending gold coins. This is Dhana Lakshmi, one of eight forms of the goddess Lakshmi, and the deity responsible for wealth, prosperity, and abundance. Her picture hangs behind the cash register in most businesses, adorned with a fresh garland of jasmine or marigolds draped across the top and curls of incense wafting nearby from the most recent puja, or worship performed for her at the beginning of every new business cycle of the day.

If there is such a thing as a "god of money," in India there are currently two main contenders.[1] The first is Lakshmi, who is dedicated to helping people increase their fortunes. The second is a local form of the god Vishnu from the southern region named Venkateshwara, whose primary temple placed within the seven hills of Tirupati is the second wealthiest religious institution today behind the Vatican. It makes sense that these two gods are married within the larger structure of the Hindu pantheon, as well as have gained many visas to the United States and other locales to be installed in temples built by Hindu communities outside of India.[2]

In addition to the gods, there are many other religious and cultural messages about wealth within the Indian context that shape attitudes toward money. On the one hand, the pursuit of wealth is one of four primary aims of life. In other contexts, holy people purposefully

Lakshmi, Hindu goddess of wealth, with rupees at her feet. (K. Zubko)

relinquish economic assets in exchange for spiritual riches. This chapter outlines perspectives on wealth in Indian contexts, as well as compares them to American mindsets. Stop and think a moment about that first dollar bill ever made by a commercial venture, signed, framed, and hanging behind the cash registers of mom and pop shops on Main Street. As a talisman of continued profit, it shares much in common with the image of Lakshmi found on the counters of sweet shops and corporate desks in India.

The Pursuit of Wealth in India

Ideas about affluence are deeply rooted in Indian culture. One of the oldest of these messages is found in the *Dharmasastras*, or law books on duty (dharma) written by and for the upper castes. In this collation is the first mention of four primary aims of life: dharma, artha, kama, and moksha. Dharma we have encountered before in the form of duties

Ingredient 7: The Pursuit of Wealth

Talisman of profit: (left) the display of Hindu gods, goddesses, and a garlanded portrait of a holy man behind the cash receipts booth at a restaurant in India; and (right) the display of the "first dollar bill" of profit and good luck bills on the wall behind the cash register in an American ice cream shop. (K. Zubko)

assigned to people based on age, gender, caste, vocation, and so on. It is an important aim of life to pursue and complete the dharma assigned to you within each lifetime. Upper-caste males for whom this text is written also are sanctioned to seek kama, or pleasure and beauty, often found in the company of women, and moksha, or spiritual salvation. The second in the list, artha, is the primary concern of this chapter. Artha holds a wide range of meanings gathered under the umbrella of "worldly success." While there are interesting tips on political strategies and the art of kingship found in texts devoted to artha, there are also suggestions for increasing one's fiscal net worth. While many of these are not appropriate strategies that today's financial advisors would propose, there is a significant message being conveyed that prosperity is a legitimate purpose in life.

In the original context, the pursuit of artha was a directive for people born into merchant, warrior, and nobility classes. Certain subcastes became associated with different types of businesses, while even particular religious backgrounds supported business as a primary vocation. The ethics of nonviolence of the Jains, for example,

Businesses as the domain of the gods: (top) shops in India named after the Hindu gods Laxmi (Lakshmi) and Krishna, and (bottom) poster prints of the Hindu gods appearing behind the cash counter at a clothing shop. (K. Zubko)

led to avoiding mercenary or warrior professions, as well as farming (tilling creatures found in the soil), in favor of developing business networks. Early seafaring Muslim traders in the southern regions of India introduced business-minded admonitions against usury, or interest, and a percentage of income to be shared among the community, both ideas following the example of the Prophet Muhammad whose wife was a successful merchant. In general, wealth is to be shared within the larger community to avoid exploitation and support those in need.

In the Hindu worldview, the acquisition of wealth is primarily considered as a form of blessings from gods and ancestors or the outcome of good karma in previous birth(s). If someone buys a new car or scooter, whether for personal or commercial use, the first destination from the showroom is invariably a temple or a place of worship to thank and seek the blessings of their favorite god or goddess before taking the vehicle home. A new house goes through an elaborate house warming ritual, *grih pravesh*, where priests invoke gods for their blessings of well-being and prosperity for the owner and invite them to take dwelling in the house that they are credited with bringing to fruition. Anything of value goes through some sort of dedication ritual before being put to use, including household appliances such as a refrigerator, a microwave oven, or electronics including TVs, stereos, home theater components, and even personal items such as a set of jewelry or new dress. This practice is still prevalent, although on the decline for items of lesser value depending on the socioeconomic class of the family.

As wealth is believed to be the result of the gods' blessings, it also means that wealth is considered transitory, and can vanish at any point. Fortunes can turn up or down based on divine favor. There are many rituals that women, in particular to the customs of their own communities, perform in order to please the gods and continue or increase the flow of blessings. For example, some Marwari women feed ants every Sunday morning. Other women keep weekly fasts on the day of the week associated with Lakshmi. In general, females are the harbingers of prosperity for the families into which they marry. There are also general practices of feeding beggars through giving alms as a quid pro quo for the continuation of gods' blessings. Unfortunately, criminals in big cities often exploit this belief through running solicitation rackets that take advantage of homeless or kidnapped children.

An important outcome of the transitory view of wealth and insecurity surrounding it is a pervasive tendency to invest in land, immovable property and gold in particular. The intent is to leave property for the next generation in order to provide financial security and to perpetuate the family name. In rural areas, wealth accumulation is reflected by ownership of agricultural land, orchards, livestock, and agricultural machinery. In urban India, wealth is stashed away in the form of houses, land, cash, gold, silver, precious stones, and gems. As the focus of wealth, property related litigation accounts for the highest number of cases in both rural and urban Indian courts, and property law in India is one of the most complicated areas of judiciary domain.[3]

As an outgrowth of the same concerns that lead to property-based wealth, India also has one of the highest savings rates in the world estimated currently at 32 percent.[4] In part, this preference to save money derives from social responsibilities and insufficient coverage of risks. Families routinely save for huge expenses, such as daughters' weddings, kids' education, family functions, funerals of parents, serious illnesses, accidents, and other family emergencies. The health care system is not properly linked to a working insurance system and the government-run hospitals are in a deplorable state. Good private hospitals are very expensive. Higher education is also not covered by federally guaranteed loans, as found in the United States. All these responsibilities are financial burdens that people carry and therefore they save money to which they have quick access. Savings, as well as property investments have been historically preferred over stock and shares until recently, since they are considered safe and liquid. Reliance was the first company credited with starting an "equity cult" by enlisting over two million shareholders for the first time in Indian history.[5] In the current urban climate, the Indian stock market is growing and savvy investors are weaving a new culture of investment in equities and mutual funds.

In the contemporary period, the pursuit of success has diffused throughout the culture. It is not wrong to better one's fortunes. While in the past, earning potential would have been restricted to the boundaries set by an allotted role in life (based on gender, caste, class, etc.); the contemporary world continues to see a breakdown in the barriers of participation and the formation of a new and diverse upwardly mobile class of hardworking individuals. A snapshot of one type of worker you might encounter might be someone like Rohan:

> *Rohan is floor manager in a BPO firm in Hyderabad but lives a very austere lifestyle. Many of his colleagues own comfortable apartments and drive nice cars but Rohan lives with his friends in a shared apartment and commutes on a scooter. He generally keeps busy with his work and avoids weekend outings with colleagues if they involve expensive bar tabs. George finds this quite intriguing. Since relocating from the Sydney office, he has been working with Rohan for over six months now and the two have become good friends. After Rohan has refused several times to join colleagues for parties, George asks him in private and is shocked to hear his story. Rohan sends money home to help his dad, who drives a three-wheeler in another town, and supports a family of four. His sister is a teacher in a primary school and is saving money for her own marriage, but Rohan knows she will need much more. Rohan's brother needs financial assistance to carry on his college studies. Rohan considers it his responsibility to ensure a good education for his brother and a decent marriage for his sister. He cannot afford to spend money on parties and prefers to maintain a simple lifestyle until his siblings are ready to fend for themselves.*

Ingredient 7: The Pursuit of Wealth   91

While people have new access to job opportunities that will help them to support their extended families in India, this is also evident in NRIs (nonresident Indians) working abroad. The World Bank reports the remittance amount to India of $52 billion in 2008; an amount that places India at the very top of the list, as members of the Indian Diaspora send money home month after month to their family and relatives.[6] If an adult child in the family obtains a good job and makes good money, one of their priorities invariably is to financially help her parents and siblings beat the cycle of poverty and wants.

The era of economic deregulation of the early 1990s is another contributing factor that opened up countless opportunities. Prior to that time, cumbersome laws made access to loans and permits very restricted, making it difficult for anyone to start a business without family money or the right contacts in government and financial institutions. There prevailed a general absence of entrepreneurship in the country due to such a tough environment, an unsupportive infrastructure, and kept business primarily confined to government, big family-run business houses and their networks. There is evidence to suggest that many people from all classes are in the process of rising within their own industries. People are taking advantage of deregulation policies, along with easier and cheaper access to technology and Internet services. As Tarun Khanna suggests, India is a nation of entrepreneurs.[7]

Indians in general keep a low profile about their wealth. However, material acquisitions are becoming more personal and function as statements of power. Until a few years ago personal jets or even chartered planes were nonexistent commodities in India. People in show business, for example, used public airlines for travel and did not display lavish lifestyles. Now things are changing and big film personalities, industrialists, and business executives prefer to fly in personal or corporate jets in total privacy and away from the public eye. The neo-rich Indians want visibility and status—so they buy expensive cars, and posh apartments, dine and wine in style and shop in glitzy malls and department stores. They are increasingly become brand conscious and love to splurge on high fashion watches, apparel, jewelry, and so on. There is a new found respect for the moneyed class due to the rise in consumerism and desire for material possessions, which in turn has created a huge market for everything under the sun in India thanks to its rising middle class numbering between 250 and 300 million and growing.

Besides an expansion of consumerism, there is also growing interests in philanthropy. While foreign philanthropists, such as Prince Charles and Bill Gates, continue to top the charts in terms of giving in India,[8] some of the leading families of industry within India are incorporating many diverse ways of reinvesting their wealth back into their local and national communities by building schools, colleges, and other social institutions. According to a 2004 study by the Global Equity Initiative of Harvard University, India has built upon religious and cultural concepts of individual, or personal forms of giving, such as *dana* (giving) in Hinduism, *bhiksha* (alms) in Buddhism, and *zakat* (prescribed offerings) in Islam, to inspire institutionalized forms of philanthropy. While still not on the same scale as what may be found in the United States, philanthropy is its own growth industry. Some of the factors contributing to the rise of a diverse array of philanthropic endeavors includes an emphasis on NPOs (nonprofit organizations) and voluntary organizations motivated through Gandhian principles of service, and the support of the primary industrial families of Tata, Birla, Godrej, Mahindra, and Bajaj, as well as foundations and programs in connection with banking (ICICI and Citibank) and technology (Infosys and Wipro) sectors. Specific foundations committed to developing philanthropic strategies and professional assistance include the Center for Advancement of Philanthropy (CAP), the Sampradaan Indian Centre for Philanthropy (SICP), and the National Foundation for India (NFI).[9] All of these indicators suggest that philanthropy is increasingly an important part of understanding views on wealth in India.

In general, Indian attitudes toward wealth are positive, enforced by religious sanctions. There are more opportunities for the entrepreneurial spirit to flourish in all sectors of society, in part borrowed from the adoption of Western models of individualism, but with an Indian flavor. As Fareed Zakaria suggests, modernization does not necessarily equate with westernization.[10] Indian ideas about how to build and manage commercial ventures will continue to grow through a mixture of past precedents and concepts, as well as new inspirations drawn from within Indian understandings of how business is done.

In God We Trust: The Self-made American and Money

Many phrases come to mind when one turns to American views on money making and wealth. "The streets are paved with gold" suggests opportunity abounds to make money easily. "He pulled himself up by his bootstraps" underscores hard work as the basis for building a fortune—something anyone can do if they put their mind to it regardless of family of birth or economic status. Indeed, American history celebrates the rise of many people who went from not owning a dime to leading financial empires of great power. Andrew Carnegie, eventually one of the largest steel tycoons, was the son of a Scottish hand-loom weaver who worked jobs in Pittsburgh as a bobbin boy in a factory, accounting clerk, and ran errands for a telegraph office before making his meteoric rise. John D. Rockefeller began life on a farm in rural western New York, only to work his way up the ladder from assistant bookkeeper to a produce merchant to oil magnate through a series of shrewd business investments.[11] These are only two of many rags-to-riches stories that emerge in the history of wealth in America and serve as models of the possible.

The mix of opportunity and hard work are part of the narrative of the self-made person that shapes American perceptions. Religious aspects contribute to this narrative in many ways, especially through a Protestant Christian work ethic that aligns industriousness with godliness. In a well-known essay written by a sociologist of religion, Max Weber, the author argues that the Calvinist underpinnings of many of the Puritans and early immigrants who went on to found the New Colonies and eventually America is an important factor in the development of capitalism. John Calvin, a Protestant reformer, had focused on a theology that rested on the total depravity of humans, among which a select group called the "elect" had already been chosen by God for salvation. Due to a predestined fate of salvation or damnation, no human could work to do anything to change their lot. Instead, hard work, industriousness, and other virtues of an ascetic-like simplicity became signs that a person was chosen to be among the "elect." The making of money, and steady increase in profits, to be saved and reinvested, but not spent on luxuries, became further proof of one's predestined salvation.[12]

According to Weber, these ideas that underscore many of the Protestant denominations that exist in the United States, led to a religious sanctioning of wealth building, as well as an ideology that creates the means for making enough capital to be able to enter into investments. This is not particular to Protestant Christians influenced by Calvin anymore, but is widespread as a part of capitalism in general. The religious landscape of America is changing fast, but the work ethic is so embedded in the self-made American narrative, it continues to be adopted by the majority of every immigrant who comes to America with a dream of a better life. If a person simply works hard and does not squander their money ("A penny saved is a penny earned"), then that person, too, has a chance of becoming a Carnegie or Rockefeller. The realities of this idealistic opportunity are more complicated than can be discussed here, especially in terms of labor practices and more recent trends in consumption of luxuries through debt. However, the main point is the belief that hard work produces a religiously sanctioned wealth still underscores business practices for many.

Other clues about American attitudes toward money can be found at the intersection with religion. In towns and cities across the United States, religious institutions used to be the tallest buildings in any given location. The spires of churches in particular rose above all other structures. Today, those spires are overshadowed by mostly financial institutions, skyscrapers of capitalism where profit may be envisioned as the highest god.

While the ties between religion and money are prominently displayed in the motto "In God We Trust" found on the dollar bill, other aspects of the American landscape reveal divinely sanctioned blessings toward accruing wealth. Mega churches have become some of the richest institutions, funding various missionary activities through polished, high-tech multimedia events and celebrity ministers that appeal to the mass public through televised and internet-streamed outlets, in addition to stadium venues. In some Christian denominations, affluence ministries accentuate messages of a god-given right to wealth as interpreted through biblical passages. Worshippers moved by a preacher delivering their sermon on this topic often bring cash forward to leave on the altar in praise of a god who provides.

While affluence ministries are becoming more common, but are not yet mainstream, the idea that suggests wealth is bestowed on those in right relationship to God is pervasive. Tithing, or giving a percentage of income to a religious organization is the most common practice that represents that all blessings, including financial, belong to God, and can be used to support the community. Individuals, as well as businesses that tithe, are on the rise, and create a range of logistical questions about how much, and to whom should this money go. Should the percentage come from gross or net profits? What charities count? Is the vision of a particular organization to help those in the local community of parishioners, or as part of a Social Gospel, include those in wider, more global circles of need as part of establishing a Kingdom of God on Earth.

Practices of tithing, according to historian James Hudnut-Beumler, were carefully reintroduced in America post–Civil War to support both local and global missions. Many of the pamphlets from this period rest on a concept of stewardship of God-given wealth that people have been bequeathed in trust, and need to be reinvested in God's work in the world.[13]

The consequences of stewardship on practices of philanthropy are far-reaching, and much like Weber's thesis, now extend into understandings of capitalism in general in the United States. While Carnegie was actually known to be stingy and a harsh man, whose fortune was only embedded into philanthropic enterprises by his heirs, the wealthiest Americans of today are expected to give back during their lives—and many do give to both religious and secular institutions. Bill Gates and Warren Buffett, among others, are at the top of the list of those making their wealth in technology and investments. In general, American views are also positive toward money, as long as this philanthropic piece is present.

Cross-Cultural Clash or Continuity in Views of Wealth?

Do American and Indian views of wealth create a tension point? Or do the views align in helpful ways? The answer lies somewhere in the middle. By becoming aware of the views in this chapter, it will help you find common ground, as well as create an approach to business management and partnerships with your Indian colleagues and teams that draws on the cultural knowledge of the role of wealth and money making in India. God-given, or divinely sanctioned wealth shows up in both worldviews, in slightly different ways, as well as creates different approaches. While in India, money as a blessing may be fleeting, and is granted according to karma, rather than hard work necessarily, in America, the impetus to save, reinvest, and live a simple life was a possible sign of salvation, at least in early American views. What people invest their money in is determined on different values. How people distribute their money is also guided on different principles in terms of philanthropic practices. By examining the motivations and belief systems underlying wealth, as well as the approaches to money making, India and America provide a useful cultural comparison that will aid those working at the investment and philanthropic levels, as well as any transactions involving the exchange of wealth and value in any form.

Summary Points

The pursuit of wealth is religiously sanctioned in both India and the United States. The sense of a divine hand that is responsible for blessings, including financial stability, is just one of many cultural messages that frame profit and money making activities in these two countries. Business decisions and workplace attitudes toward profit are influenced in part by the authority and meaning derived from these faith-based convictions.

The upwardly mobile middle class is diverse, young, and committed to change. New opportunities created by economic deregulation and globalization has led to a surge of employment that draws on the best and brightest of India's young professionals. Hard work, long hours, and innovation are key descriptors of this population that has begun to break through class and gender barriers.

Savings and investment in property have been preferred in the past, although stocks are on the rise. Due to the need for easy access to money to cover major family expenses such as marriages and education, assets existed in properties that secured the long-term well-being of the family or in more liquid forms. A younger professional population is now exploring a wider portfolio of options, once the family's immediate expenses are stabilized.

Philanthropy in both India and the United States arise out of religious and social principles. Philanthropy in India is a budding field, with many strong examples in place based on Gandhian ideals of service, along with other religious models of giving.

Chapter 10

Ingredient 8: The Original Business Contract

We live in a world surrounded by transactions and contracts. Transactions are the most basic and unwritten form of contracts we get in and out of on a regular basis without even consciously being aware of them. When you hire a cab for a ride an unwritten contract is established between you and the driver. He takes you to your destination and at the end of your journey you pay him tacitly at the rates fixed by the city. We sign more clearly defined and formal contracts for mobile phones, credit cards, utilities, rent, mortgage, car, and so on. Normally the contracts get executed without much fuss but occasionally people run into problems when one of the parties fails to fulfill stated responsibilities or defaults on obligations. The factor that is most often missed when people from different cultures enter into a contract is the underlying unspoken cultural expectations of what that relationship entails. People fail to raise certain concerns or provide information that within their own cultures is assumed to be part of a contractual relationship.

One important model for understanding the dynamics of contracts in India originates in the ancient practice of fire sacrifice. Priests make offerings into a fire on behalf of a petitioner not as a form of prayer or expression of gratitude, but in order to create a binding, nonnegotiable contract between humans and gods. In contemporary India, priests still perform fire sacrifices to a lesser degree for special religious events, demonstrating its long-standing foothold in the culture. This chapter explores the different components of this ritual to expose some of the unstated cross-cultural expectations created between parties participating in formal and informal agreements today in the Indian context.

The Birth of Middle Management

In the Vedic period, fire sacrifice served as the primary form of contract between humans and the gods. This was not a channel of direct

Fire sacrifice being conducted by local priests at a Hindu temple in Greensboro, North Carolina, in 2009. (K. Zubko)

communication, but required intermediaries. A person who wanted to make a request to the gods hired a priest to initiate and carry through on all the requirements to set up the connection. A skillful priest is one who had been properly trained in the Vedic scriptures that contained both the instructions and hymns to be chanted for the ritual. Successful priests who produced efficacious results were in high demand.

The priests are not the only intermediaries in this situation. The other important middleman is the fire that transforms the offerings into smoke. The priests spend a good portion of the ritual addressing the god Agni, or fire itself, without which the offerings (flowers, milk, *ghee* or clarified butter, etc.) and requests would never physically rise to reach the intended recipients.

In Indian business contexts, intermediaries are a necessary component of contract negotiations. Rather than dealing directly with the primary party, a designated representative may be sent instead, as part of cultural protocol. This is not an unknown practice in America, where powerful lobbyists make the rounds in the corridors of power in Washington on behalf of countries, causes, and corporations whose interests they represent.

The scenario is a little murky in India and one has to tread with a lot of caution. In the absence of legally recognized lobbying firms, many of the intermediaries operate in an underground network. People of all kinds participate in intermediary activities ranging from Members of Parliament, c-level executives, and business magnates to low-paid assistants in a government job. Sometimes the job title or position of a person can be misleading in terms of power or influence he or she may be able to exercise. Both Indian politics and business are replete with tales of friends, advisors, wives, sidekicks, and even mistresses wielding enormous influence in business deals and contracts. Part of setting up a contract in India is to find out who the appropriate intermediaries are that you need to interface with in order to get the job done.

> *John works as a business development manager for a European sales promotion and event management company in Mumbai. He is excited about clinching a deal for a 10-city road event featuring an Indian appliance company. The marketing director likes his proposal and cost estimates and advises him to come back with final figures and documents. However, when he shows up on the appointed date and time he is ushered into the office of the finance director who rejects his proposal on cost grounds. He tries to reason with him and offers to rework costs but to no avail. Puzzled, John speaks to the marketing director. He expresses his inability to do anything to help John out since finance makes the final call on expenses. Soon John also finds out that the finance director is the co-owner of the company and brother of the president. In his earlier visits and presentations John interacts only with the marketing director and his colleagues and never bothers to probe into or understand the business hierarchy and role of intermediaries to all offices involved in a decision.*

John hit a major roadblock because he was under the assumption that the original colleague in marketing that showed enthusiasm for the project and encouraged creating a proposal would be involved in ushering the project through all the necessary levels of bureaucracy. Because of the division of labor and rules of hierarchy, it is important to inquire and meet with any other parties involved in the decision-making process through a designated intermediary who can bridge all those different offices smoothly.

Contracts often are signed at the end of a very prolonged process. This is especially true when multiple parties vie with each other to win the contract through a bidding process. Besides doing the laborious documentation work, the competing parties also need to interact with several people and go through many steps and prerequisites along the way. This process can be even more cumbersome if the contract is being awarded by a government corporation. However, by extending yourself to work with intermediaries along each step of the process, you gain expertise and advice that can make the difference in being awarded contracts.

> *Brenda works as the project director for a U.S. earth-moving equipment company in Chennai. Her company bids for large road construction projects. Though the final contract will be signed between her company and the government, Brenda understands the role of intermediary officials in the process. These officials screen, evaluate, and suggest clarifications to the proposals and call the bidding parties for meetings to make presentations. Before submitting her bid, Brenda establishes contact with the officials involved in the process. In several meetings with these officials, Brenda and her team discuss the strengths of her company, the skill sets of her team members, as well as other projects her company successfully completed in India and neighboring regions in the past five years. Brenda invites the intermediaries to the site office for a physical verification of infrastructure, equipment, inventory, and other support systems.*
>
> *The officials appreciate Brenda's sincere and proactive approach. They offer valuable advice that helps Brenda in the documentation process and in developing competitive cost estimates for the project. It also helps her pick the projects that best match with the strengths of the resources and expertise of the engineers in the company. Hard work eventually bears fruit and Brenda's company wins three out of five bids on large road construction projects.*

Finding those intermediaries that are the most helpful is often by word of mouth—there is no directory that can provide you this information. Asking for a liaison, yet another type of intermediary, is a crucial first step. A liaison is someone who can affirm the "credentials of experience" of all the other intermediaries and put you in touch with all the right people no matter what the contract is you are seeking.

Appropriate Requests: Order and Abundance

Priests perform fire sacrifices to create contracts for particular reasons. In general, these reasons could be characterized as creating a state of order. Order is defined by every microcosmic structure being in right relationship to the cosmos, from the individual and family level to kingdoms and society. A state of order also means managing any major change to that order, as well as increasing a state of abundance. Types of appropriate requests include the birth of a son to carry on the family lineage, blessings on a new undertaking, such as victory in an upcoming battle, or good growing conditions for crops. Requests that do not fall into this range were not considered important.

Contracts are thought to align things for the good of both parties. If it brings order to the relationship and has the intent of creating abundance, the contract is considered valid, and under this model, religiously sanctioned. If any part of the contract does not have this intent, it goes against the very nature of the function of a contract. What are the functions of the contracts you are making? Why are you entering into a particular contract? How does that contract change in order to create more alignment between provider services and fulfilling the most immediate and ever-changing needs of clients?

A U.S. telecommunications company that partners with an Indian IT company for its billing and customer services faces a unique problem. Over the years the ranks of Spanish speaking customers has been growing rapidly and the management is now considering bilingual statements of bills (online and paper) and hiring language proficient resources to service them better. The Indian IT partner in Hyderabad currently has no employees that speak Spanish. With the contract set to expire within the year, the U.S. company is under pressure to look for alternative business partners that can also offer Spanish language support.

When Karen, VP, International Business brings this concern up for discussion during a business review meeting in India, Sundar Rajan, the CEO of the Indian company promises to look into plausible solutions right away. Sundar apprises his colleague Manju Nath in the Mexico City office of his business problem and requests him to check whether associates working there are open to relocating to India on a long-term basis. Fortunately, five associates express their willingness to live and work in India. Excited, Sundar makes the necessary arrangements for their immigration, visa, travel and everything else and after four weeks they land in India. Sundar informs Karen of the new possibility for language services and offers to make the transition six months before the contract expires without asking for any extra money. Karen saves resources by avoiding a new bidding process for IT support and happily renews the contract as the relationship between the companies grows stronger. This also enables Sundar to successfully develop the capability to service other Spanish language customers by leveraging the language skills of his Mexican associates and expanding language training to hundreds of Indian employees. In time, Sundar wins lucrative business contracts from other U.S. and European companies because of the Spanish language support advantage.

Sundar's foresight and timely actions to meet the immediate and upcoming needs of his telecommunications client set a clear path for exactly what type of support services would be available under a continuing contract, and leads to a win-win situation for all parties involved in the development of a stronger working relationship between the companies. This is an ideal and sustainable contract due to order and abundance working hand in hand.

Timing, Proper Performance, and the Power of the Verbal Word

Hiring the right priest for the job is important for several reasons. The first thing the chosen priest must do is determine the right time and place for the ritual to occur in alignment with the position of the stars. People may say that they "thank their lucky stars" when something good happens or crisis is avoided. In consulting the star positions in India in order to fix the details for the fire sacrifice, priests increase the potential for a successful request. Any new undertaking, whether a marriage or new business, will officially start at designated times and dates.

Besides timing, the words and actions of this ritual, if performed correctly, create a compulsory response from the gods, who have to fulfill the contract without exception. There is an extremely powerful cultural message here about the performance of a contract. Content alone is not the only factor. It is also the way the content is carried out in tone, intent, and spirit. If a priest fumbles the intonation of a word, or chooses the wrong offering, these mistakes create loopholes that allow the gods to get out of their obligations. It is the execution that creates and fulfills the requirements of the relationship.

In general, words on paper are not as binding as a verbal statement or gesture of commitment to an agreed course of action. Unlike

American firms, who would deliver as per the terms of a contract, Indian companies may choose to go beyond the letter of a contract and try to follow its spirit in the hope of satisfying the customer and establishing a long-lasting enduring relationship.

> *A U.S.-based department store chain hires a Mumbai-based IT company to develop custom software to improve its sales productivity and customer services. A contract is signed after mutual agreement of terms and conditions and development work gets underway. During the midway review of the product the customer expresses how some extra features and capabilities, if incorporated in the software, would make the software better and more useful to the firm. The Indian company changes the scope of the project and develops all the extra features and capabilities in its final product with a view to making the customer satisfied without requesting a revision in the formal terms of the contract. It is a cultural assumption that the customer will revise the contract and pay for extra work. The Indian company never feels constrained by the sanctity of the written word, especially when it would limit fulfilling the changing needs of the client. Taking a more long-term approach to nurturing a business relationship, the Indian company assumes that the contract can be renegotiated at any stage. While this flexibility is viewed as a positive approach that stays on the cutting edge with clients without the hassle of reworking formal agreements, the perceived informality can create misunderstandings if the relationship is not on the same page.*

In some contexts, the paper trail of required permits and signatures is overwhelmingly bureaucratic, while in other contexts, a written agreement is still viewed with suspicion. The promise to fulfill an obligation (i.e., giving a "word" to do something) has been equivalent to a binding contract. In the Indian epic *Ramayana*, Tulsidas composes a Hindi couplet on the value of a "word": "*Raghukul riti sada chali aayi, prana jayi par vachan na jayi.*" (It has been a time-honored tradition in Rama's illustrious family to keep one's word or promise at any cost and is even worth dying for.)

Informal contracts are a way of life at the daily level in India. Every building or household has a designated newspaper agent, grocery shop, iron press man, milk vendor, and so on and they are very territorial. They get into fights when other vendors and suppliers try to entice their customers away. Often the same set of vendors has been providing service to a particular family for years, sometimes for generations.

They become part of the family and are even invited to social events, such as weddings. With family wealth often invested in gold, the family jeweler is one example of an indispensible vendor who often works by way of informal contracts:

> *In many jewelry stores in India, the jeweler usually offers a discount if you do not insist on receiving a genuine sales receipts (pacca). Though he wants to save on his taxes he would try to encourage your compliance by offering a sales discount and receipt made in hand (kacha). He would vouch for the sanctity of his verbal receipt and you could rest assured that he would always honor its terms. This creates a form of an unwritten contract between the two parties. While the customer receives a good bargain as part of entering into this informal arrangement the jeweler potentially establishes a long-term relationship through a single sale. By fulfilling his side of the contract the jeweler is almost sure of serving the customer and his friends and relatives in the future by way of repeat sales and referrals. As long as both sides fulfill their obligations and are receiving good value the relationship continues and grows in strength.*

Even in modern times when most business and government work is conducted through written documents, the tradition of verbal, informal transactions is still widely prevalent in India. In general, contracts are perceived more as personally, socially, and morally binding obligations rather than simply fulfilling written terms.

Be mindful that your actions will be interpreted even more closely than written statements or signed documents. The more attention paid to how contracts are executed, and incorporation of gestures that follow the spirit of the contract, the more people will be compelled to hold up their end of the agreement.

Exchange, Compliance, and Repeat Business

The outcome of a successful fire sacrifice is not just in the response of the gods, it is also in setting up a relationship of exchange that invites further transactions. The correct actions of the priest on behalf of the sponsor create the circumstances for contract fulfillment. Actions of the gods proceed in exchange for the offerings and words performed. Often these words include a vow to complete another ritual action on behalf of the god once the job is complete—a spiritual COD. The most common vow is to take a pilgrimage, or make offerings at a particular temple.

Ingredient 8: The Original Business Contract 105

In a cultural sense, this means that the cycle of exchange is never really complete once the business relationship has been set up. This is a good thing for both parties, as the gods receive a continuous supply of offerings, and humans, in theory, see their requests granted. If not, the contract is broken and another god is sought for partnership. If successful, the creation of a business contract extends beyond into a long-standing relationship.

> *In the winter months, weavers from Kashmir, Himachal Pradesh, and other colder northern regions of India fan throughout the rest of India with their woolen products and sell them by moving door to door. In several cases when the customers are not able to pay the full amount for the goods, they offer to collect money in installments during the time of their stay. There is no written contract. They simply rely on the goodwill and trust of their customers and in exchange they are able to make their sale and build a relationship with the customers and their friends. The next season they are welcome to build off of repeat business through their established network.*

The same dynamic is at work in all levels of industry, with the underlying motivation being one of developing trust and furthering relationships to ensure continued business transactions. For example, predicting and addressing the needs of a client is a primary way of sustaining the longevity of a working business partnership:

> *The BPO and IT industry have raised a newer concern in business contracts—that of privacy protection since customer data and personal information are shared between partners. Since employees working in these establishments work in a variety of situations such as processing of medical records, credit card bills, mortgage loan applications, insurance claims, and so on where they have access to sensitive personal information many countries have passed data protection laws that cover their business partners or incorporated such clauses into their contract documents.*
>
> *Culturally, privacy has a low priority among Indians and is construed more in terms of private space rather than personal information. Most Indians have a large family, which often extends to include distant relatives, and are brought up with little or no privacy. However they grow up with a lot of trust for each other and feel safe confiding in their family and friends. This attitude toward privacy also applies to the personal information of their colleagues and customers to which they*

have access. It is no surprise then that India has a near stellar record in data security.

Anand Naidu works as the COO of an IT services company in Bangalore. He is very particular about data security issues. To ensure continued patronage of his clientele, he installs surveillance equipment and security systems that inspire confidence in his partners. His company adheres to a zero tolerance policy on data matters and Anand personally insists on extensive data security clauses in all his contracts, which may or may not be required by law or demanded by his business partners. He willingly transfers the onus on his company and colleagues for the personal information of the customers they are privileged to service. Anand looks at his business relationships not merely as revenue streams but as an integral part of his business and a reflection on his company's mission and goal of executing his side of the deal with integrity, transparency, and the highest standards of professional excellence.

Summary Points

The fire sacrifice, as one of the oldest contracts performed in India, illuminates many important features at work in contractual relationships today. Keeping these pointers in mind will help you navigate cultural assumptions within transactions and prevent misunderstandings.

- **Intermediaries are part of creating contracts.** Part of setting up a contract in India is to find out who the appropriate intermediaries are that you need to interface with in order to get the job done. This allows for people at different and similar ranks to interface smoothly and with appropriate levels of respect.
- **The primary purpose of contracts is to create order and increase assets.** In an ideal contract, the clarifying of the needs and services of both parties in relationship with each other leads to a win-win situation that is mutually beneficial. Otherwise, the contract has inherent weaknesses that will not sustain the relationship over time.
- **Actions and words speak louder than written documents.** While in government domains, obtaining permits and other written documents is a full-time job, and can be a major source of delays if not all the right pieces of paper and signatures are collected, at the daily level informal verbal contracts are more prevalent. A person's word carries more weight in the context of long-term relationships.

Based on accurate performance, compliance is expected. If services or obligations are not fulfilled, this would be grounds to break a contract and seek a more efficacious business partnership. As with all contracts, both sides are expected to fulfill the terms of the agreement, however in India, attention is also paid to how the obligations are fulfilled in spirit.

A contract symbolizes an ongoing relationship of exchange. Agreements with your Indian business colleagues and partners are opportunities to build a track record of reliable, consistent interactions. Creating trust and reciprocity leads to further business transactions. Think through the consequences of breaking any contract obligations, as they will do more long-term damage to the overall relationship within the Indian business context.

Chapter 11

Ingredient 9: Nonconfrontational Negotiation

Sylvia, a senior technology executive with an MNC based in Boston, arrives in Mumbai to lead and supervise a software project with an Indian IT partner. Prior to her arrival, she reaches a common understanding on all the project modules and shell design concepts with her Indian counterpart and his team over several phone discussions and web ex presentations. However, in her early meetings in Mumbai, one thing that puzzles her the most is the shaking of heads from side to side by many of her Indian colleagues. She translates this body language as disagreement and alerts Boston, but remains confused since no one raises any direct objection or challenges her point of view. In response, Sylvia attempts to propose a few slight modifications to see if it will elicit a more direct yes or no. This time the head nodding is accompanied by a "we'll see." She receives frantic calls from Boston expressing deep concern over the prospects of cost escalation if the scope of the project undergoes any change. Sylvia is not sure where the project stands.

Sylvia is caught in a "lost in translation" moment. As she begins to observe more interactions around her in the markets, on trains, and among her Indian colleagues, she begins to realize that the head nodding from side to side, which means "no" in the United States, actually takes on a range of meanings in India—Yes, I like that, I agree with you, and even a form of greeting. Sylvia also witnesses an exchange in which an Indian colleague responded to a request with a "we'll see," instead of "no," even though she was aware that the resources for the request were not available. Sylvia realizes that she has misread these local gestures, and informs her bosses in Boston that everything is on track. Modifications are in fact not necessary and even unwanted.

Learning how to negotiate well is part talent and part skill. When trying to negotiate across cultures, the skills required include being able to modify and read local gestures—both nonverbal and verbal. One of the most important cultural templates that inform negotiation styles in India to varying degrees is the principle of ahimsa, or nonviolence. While not the only model for negotiations, ahimsa is one way to explain why a direct "no" is perceived as rude, an unnecessary form of confrontation, and leaves out the possibility for change.

While ahimsa is found within the belief systems and practices of many of the denominations of Hinduism, Buddhism, and Jain religions, one of the greatest and well-known expressions of ahimsa may be attributed to Mohandas K. Gandhi, also known as "Mahatma," or great soul. His negotiation approach in working toward Indian political and economic independence from the British Empire utilized aspects of ahimsa to assert a powerful force not based on manipulation, brutality, or anger. Not everyone possesses the charisma and determination of Gandhi, however, the influence of ahimsa experienced through religious convictions and exemplary leaders infuses the mindset of many whom you will encounter within contexts of negotiation. This chapter identifies and illustrates how principles of ahimsa may be at work in your next business meeting.

Ahimsa in Religious and Cultural Practices

Many of the religions of India see ahimsa as a pillar that guides human actions in the world. Both Buddhism and Jainism, which began in the sixth century B.C.E., introduce important aspects of nonviolence toward self and others into the culture. In the Jain tradition, for example, ahimsa is the first of five ethical vows taken by monks, nuns, as well as the everyday Jain practitioner. The vow to refrain from physical, as well as more subtle emotional and mental acts of violence (feeling hate or thinking bad thoughts about a person), helps people avoid the worldly and spiritual consequences of such actions. The Buddha advocates for moderation—not fasting your body away for the sake of spiritual realization, or indulging too heavily in luxuries. Compassion becomes the guideline for nonviolence. Even as Buddhism spreads outside of India, its tenets promoted peaceful coexistence, along with a new basis for political alliances. Travel accounts written by Buddhist monks Fa-Hien, and Huen-Tsang from China, Megasthenes from Greece, and several others stand proof of India's friendly relations with the then existing kingdoms and its somewhat pacifist demeanor.[1]

Mahatma Gandhi, one of the most influential leaders to shape contemporary Indian ways of being, learned about ahimsa in part through spending his youth among Jain neighbors. Influenced also by Christian pacifist groups and ideas from the Sermon on the Mount,[2] Gandhi developed techniques that worked toward increasing human and civil rights, coining the term *satyagraha*, or a grasping of the truth of all sides.[3] The pursuit of truth lends itself to intentional, conscious acts guided by ahimsa. Nonviolent does not mean being passive or inactive. Instead, these techniques that have been adopted in many contexts around the globe include demonstrations, strikes, boycotts, and forms of active noncooperation as a form of resistance. Some examples include Martin Luther King, Jr. fighting for civil rights, Nelson Mandela and Desmond Tutu working against apartheid in South Africa, the Dalai Lama's struggle for a free Tibet, and Aung San Suu Kyi and Mir-Hossein Mosavi's championing for democratic rights in Myanmar and Iran, respectively. Not all of these people succeed in attaining all of their objectives, but it inevitably brings about the start of deliberations at a new level. Satyagraha puts ahimsa into action, as a foundation for negotiation.

There are several points that Gandhi expanded upon in terms of the application of ahimsa, as the "only true force in life."[4] In business relationships, you may recognize this approach in others, or may garner respect by incorporating some of this mindset into a range of contexts. Whether you are working out the details of an employee contract or facilitating the resolution of a conflict, ahimsa is capable of improving both the process and long-term outcomes of your negotiation strategy.

Ahimsa in Business: Asking (and Answering) the Larger Questions of Context

One of the best ways to illustrate how ahimsa influences different aspects of negotiation is to breakdown the different questions of context. While each context will have its own unique factors that must be taken into account, the following suggest how ahimsa affects the larger questions.

Who?

This question refers to you and all parties involved. It is important to identify not only who you are negotiating with, but more importantly, how do you characterize the people with whom you are negotiating? With ahimsa, the answer rests in your perspective. Any discrepancies in levels of power and authority should not matter, as long as people are treated with respect, and no one takes advantage of any perceived weaknesses or vulnerabilities. Rather than see people as an "other," "enemy," or "competitor," the key is to envision people as partners who can work together toward shared goals.[5] All points of view should be part of the conversation.[6] With ahimsa, the choice of how you approach the people in the room is your responsibility.

Admittedly, this is an ideal view, as stronger partners take advantage of weaker ones all the time. This causes undue stress on partnerships and a waste of time and resources when weaker partners have to ask for revisions or even annulments in order to gain better deals. If the partnership is negotiated from the beginning in terms of shared benefits, both partners win, as seen in the following case study.

> *A New Delhi based U.S. company that sells office equipment and consumer electronics starts negotiations with a select group of five potential local businesses for a retail partnership. In this arrangement, the local partner is responsible only for sales, while the larger company remains responsible for warrantees, repairs, and services. The best possible match emerges with a retailer of imported electronics goods, Everest Electronics. Even though Everest is small, its managers show a willingness to pursue aggressive sales targets and offers to expand the network in the city based on its sales performance. In order to fully meet those needs, Everest asks for training support for its sales personnel and a dedicated manager from the company as a liaison. In exchange, the larger company demands a dedicated floor area and joint sharing of local advertising and promotions. Partners agree on an incremental commission structure linked to quarterly and annual sales performance as the basis of support for expansion. Everest leverages its deep product knowledge and its loyal customer base to produce excellent sales results month after month. In time, Everest has built a network of 25 retail outlets in the city and the neighboring region and earns a preferred partner status. The company could not have asked for a more cost-efficient and reliable channel to expand its local sales network. Even though the U.S. company could buy out Everest at any point, it is to both partners benefit to remain in a retail partnership agreement.*

When?

In American culture, the phrase "time is of the essence" refers to a culture of "now," "ASAP," and an expectation of tasks being completed

Ingredient 9: Nonconfrontational Negotiation

as quickly as possible. Ahimsa works on a different timeline, focusing on long-term solutions. Time in general is not pressing. Negotiating a contract within a certain timeframe is not important, and may even be perceived as a pressure tactic. If something has not existed for centuries, a few more months does not matter. In addition, factors that are out of the control of your business partners, such as government bureaucracies, including customs and port procedures, may affect deadlines, and should be heeded as part of doing business in India. This means that deadlines may not hold weight, and patience is required for people who are trained to speed toward an outcome. Instead, all outcomes are created as part of the partnering process together. Setting tentative deadlines or ones that account for unexpected factors is a helpful strategy that can ease tension in a contractual relationship, otherwise the following consequences may occur.

> *Jerry, a merchandise buyer for a leading U.S. clothing chain, feels frustrated when talks get stalemated on the issue of shipment schedules and turnovers with an Indian apparel company, Aquarius Exports. Jerry wants a time commitment that would work well with his company's sales forecast and U.S. seasonal cycles. The Aquarius CEO, Raghu Nair, assures Jerry that Aquarius will do everything in its power to comply with his terms, but is unable to commit to a timeline since his shipping company depends on government officials for verification and dispatching of its export consignments. On occasion, cases get stuck in bureaucratic red tape leading to further delays. Raghu does not want to promise Jerry something that is not in his hands. Jerry does not feel disposed to working out a timeframe that provides for extra time to accommodate the shipping port uncertainties. Negotiations break down and put an end to what could have been a fruitful partnership.*

What?

Negotiations are happening all the time around us, whether it is the kids in the sandbox deciding on how to share toys or government officials working out trade agreements. But what exactly is at the heart of a negotiation? What do we really want? On the surface, it may be products, services, or types of behavior. Underneath these details, when people negotiate, according to a Gandhian interpretation, they ideally need to reach an agreement that works for all participants involved. In order to achieve a workable outcome, negotiations must center on mutual cooperation that seeks out and utilizes the truth of all sides. For example,

> *Tina is a happy homemaker with two adorable toddlers. Life is wonderful until her husband, Gary, loses his job at the investment bank and expenses slowly start to mount. Over the next few months they begin to default on credit card payments, while trying to cover their home mortgage, car loan, and utilities. Collection agents begin to call, utilizing increasing threats to coerce payment. After putting up with the insults and embarrassment, Tina and Gary speak to their attorney friend Rachel for help. Rachel impresses upon the credit card companies that Tina and Gary want to repay every penny they owe, but they need time to find new sources of income. She successfully negotiates a 120-day freeze period and a reasonable reduction in interest rates. After a few months Gary finds a new job and Tina gets a license to start a home daycare center. Income starts to trickle in, they keep a check on their expenses, and begin to pay off their debts.*

This is a dire situation in which life circumstances make a binding contract untenable in the short term. Tina and Gary want to pay their debts, but are temporarily unable. The bank wants its payment. In trying to negotiate a middle path, both sides have to be flexible. The bank needs to allow Tina and Gary a chance to create income without the threat of loss of shelter for them and their two children, and even transportation to find and get to work. Tiny and Gary may have to make new agreements, but they should not be coercive or unreasonable. This way the bank will eventually begin receiving payments again, rather than losing that income completely.

How?

Intimidation, or any form of manipulation, will not work in the long term to get what you want according to this principle. This includes threats, bullying, blackmailing, as well as all sorts of subtle coercive methods that will backfire eventually. Negotiators who work under the motto "the means justify the end" will not be as successful in this context. Instead, the means and the end are the same.[7] An agreement reached under threat weakens the long-term viability of the outcome, and vice versa. A solid agreement is in direct proportion to the integrity of the actions taken during the negotiation process, as illustrated in the following example.

> *In the 1990s, a rising star of the Indian IT sector faced a moral dilemma. A multinational global conglomerate that accounted for a quarter of*

its revenue demanded discounted billing. The Indian IT company felt slighted because it was an attempt to exploit its revenue dependence on the MNC. It consulted other IT services companies and tried to raise a collective voice against the unethical threat, but in the end was left alone without any partners. No one wanted to hurt their own business interests and relationship with the global company. Refusing to cooperate with this coercive tactic, the Indian IT company walked away from the MNC's business and informed its shareholders of its decision to avoid any severe beating of its share prices. Shareholders respected the company for taking a stand and retained their stock. Today, that IT company is one of the 100 largest and fastest growing IT companies in the world.

In seeking truth, according to Gandhi, one must be fearless in his/her convictions.[8] To compromise on what is truth for you is not an act of ahimsa, since giving something up by either or both parties can leave a lingering feeling of defeat. In his analysis of Gandhian principles, Mark Juergensmeyer, a scholar of religion and conflict, suggests that forced victories, accommodation, compromise, arbitration, and law are all possible effective negotiation approaches with proven track records, and yet each of these approaches do not ideally satisfy everyone involved. Instead, satyagraha, as the application of ahimsa, creates a process in which a new mutually beneficial solution or agreement is created that avoids either side feeling slighted.[9]

Where?

Negotiations happen in India always within a space of hospitality, whether in an office or home. You are still a guest and your Indian business partners or team members are hosts. As a guest, any overt displays of disagreement with you or denial of your comfort would be considered rude coming from a host. Ahimsa only reinforces this attitude. Attempting to negotiate within this framework of hospitality can be a challenge, as the needs of both parties are not always directly put on the table. Seeking the truth of both sides must be done within a hospitable atmosphere that not only refers to the actual space, but also a welcoming attitude of being willing to work together.

Why?

A Gandhian approach may seem more an ideal, than an actual practice, however, the number one reason to utilize ahimsa is because it has the potential to transform relationships into sustainable, working partnerships.[10] Putting in the effort now has long-term payoffs. For example, several IT services companies including Infosys pride themselves on their long-term relationships with their U.S. and European clients. Over 90 percent of Infosys's revenue comes from its existing clients.[11]

Two of the top experts in the field of negotiation, Roger Fisher and William Ury, suggest focusing on the principles, not the person.[12] This approach aligns with ahimsa, especially in terms of not engaging in personal attacks. Through a Gandhian perspective, by following the principle of ahimsa, it ultimately places people back at the center of a negotiation. When people are not at the center of a relationship or agreement, the situation is vulnerable to volatility and losses for all sides, as evidenced in the following example:

> *In January 2008, Tata Nano, the eagerly awaited world's cheapest car made news for all the wrong reasons. The government of West Bengal had allotted a 1,000 acre plot in Singur to Tata for building the manufacturing plant. The rollout was scheduled for October 2009. But suddenly Singur witnessed a series of violent protests and demonstrations against the state government, which had forcibly acquired agricultural land from farmers for the factory without adequate compensation. Many farmers lost their only means of livelihood against their will, or were left without resources to build a new life. Demonstrations soon acquired a political color and became a standoff between the ruling party and the opposition. Protests grew in intensity and eventually forced Tata to abandon the project altogether since it started posing serious threat to the lives and security of employees of the company, as well as those of vendors and suppliers. Tata shifted its base to another state and rolled out its first Nano after a six-month delay in March 2009. Farmers in West Bengal are still fighting for their rights and return of their land from the state government.*

The state government bartered away the rights of powerless farmers to Tata in order to earn a industry-friendly tag but in the process not only hurt its own people and slapped a loss of millions to Tata but also inflicted a terrible blow to the image of the state and its chances of attracting investments from local or foreign investors. If a different type of negotiation had been arranged that did not take advantage of the power differential, another outcome may have been possible for all the people involved. If given the opportunity, farmers may have decided to give their consent to sell their land for a fair compensation at market rates and a stake in the company. In this case, the story would have been different.

Critique of Ahimsa

Utilizing ahimsa as a negotiation strategy is not without its fault lines or critiques. For example, what happens if one side works within the principles of ahimsa, and the other side does not? Is there any situation that is too big to approach through ahimsa? Is any degree of coercion ever justified?

In short, the answers to all these questions require an exploratory attitude and reveal the many gray areas that must be worked through in each context. For example, at the outset, coercion is never acceptable. However, what is more important is to be sensitive to what might feel like coercion—it will look different to different people. Even Gandhi has been critiqued by people who noted that many of the techniques of satyagraha have coercive elements, even if on subtle emotional levels (such as with fasting).[13] Intent is important here.

In all cases, persistence and patience are key qualities, as ahimsa is an approach that ideally can be useful in all situations, even with challenges of size or resistant partners. In Mark Juergensmeyer's analysis, tentative solutions can be forwarded until larger shared agreements can be reached.[14] Proceed with identifiable truths as a way of convincing negotiation partners of potential outcomes that benefit them as well, as illustrated in the following case.

> *Rajat is happy to be back in India after an interlude of 10 years that he spent studying for his MBA and working in senior positions in marketing and business planning at the leading MNCs in the United States. He interviews for a senior management role with an Asian Consumer Durables giant that is just entering the Indian market. He is excited to leverage his skills to design a successful business strategy. The company offers Rajat the job, but wants to hire him at a lower level because he has been away from India for 10 years. Rajat feels he deserves a higher position, so he negotiates with the company for a probationary period of six months to prove his worth, with promotion if satisfied then, rather than the normal timeline of three years.*
>
> *Two weeks into his job Rajat finds several anomalies in the business model and discreetly sets up time with the president to present his suggestions. The company had hired separate functional heads for sales and*

marketing that Rajat identifies as causing unnecessary conflicts between the two departments. A single sales and marketing team headed by one person will be more cohesive and cost-efficient. Similarly the pay structure for sales personnel designed by HR appears flawed. It offers an above industry base pay and small commissions on sales—not a very challenging and motivating scenario. Rajat proposes to reverse it—a low base pay and commissions proportionate to sales performance divided into bands. This strategy motivates higher sales through a higher pay packet, but also puts pressure on average performers to do better or leave.

The president invites him to present his revised business model before the board, which unequivocally endorses it. Within three months Rajat's new business model produces impressive results—revenue soars by 40 percent and sales productivity almost doubles. The company duly recognizes Rajat's contribution and he gets elevated to the position he deserves. He looks at his original employment contract as a platform, or a tentative solution, to demonstrate his worth to the company.

Rajat's case study demonstrates that anything is possible, even if it takes time and graduated steps as part of the negotiation process.

In all, following the practice of asking and answering the questions of context in any situation through the lens of ahimsa is a tool that can work to the advantage of all participating parties. Experiment with it and see how it works for you!

Summary Points

People are partners, not opponents. If a negotiation is begun with the mindset that people are on opposite sides, an unnecessary gap is created. It can be more difficult to work back toward common goals that benefit all parties involved. In short, the principle of ahimsa keeps people in mind.

Intimidation or any other manipulative means do not justify the end. If a long-term relationship is a desirable goal, the approaches people engage in during negotiation should support and encourage further sustainable interactions.

Seek truth in all sides without compromise. A negotiation approach that enlists an exploration of multiple perspectives, and takes them seriously, leads to the creation of a solid, shared outcome with fewer weaknesses.

Chapter 12

Ingredient 10: Cultural Views of Time and Space

Location: Headquarters of an Indian conglomerate in NOIDA with investments in telecom, insurance, and retail

The office contains an air of excitement this morning. The corporation is scheduled to finally formalize its relationship with a reputed American insurance company, after months of hard work. The delegation arrives 15 minutes early for the time that has been appointed for signing the contract at 10:30 in the morning. They are ushered into the boardroom where they meet other board members over snacks and tea, while everyone waits for the CEO, Narendra Mohan, to arrive. Narendra leaves home early to visit his family priest for blessings for the new business partnership on his way to work. But the ritual takes more time than he thought it would, and he arrives half an hour late. Before he greets the delegates, he makes sure his assistant removes the boxes of supplies that have been carelessly left to block a part of the door leading into the boardroom. Once the way is completely clear, he enters and apologizes for the delay and inconvenience caused to the delegates. The room remains heavy for some time as a couple of them indirectly express their displeasure for being made to wait. Narendra discreetly makes sure to sit in the southwest corner of the table, and invites his partners to take the seats next to him, rather than across from him. Eventually everyone lightens up, and the agreement is signed.

Narendra feels he may have annoyed his new partners. He knew the timeframe the contract should be signed in for the best possible relationship was between 10:30 and 11:30 A.M. In addition, he made sure, by the removal of boxes and the organization of seating, to give the highest possible chances to metaphorically remove potential obstacles, and reinforce setting up an egalitarian, versus hierarchal relationship. His late arrival may have been misconstrued as disrespect, which was not his intent. All that he did was for the best possible alignment in the interest of both parties.

The clock hanging on the wall, ticking away each minute of the work day may seem the same no matter what time zone you find yourself in. Similarly, a room filled with desks divided into individualized cubicles may seem like any other company workspace. This is true except for when it comes to cultural interpretations of time and space. Assumptions about how time should be "spent" or how space is divided can produce unexpected clashes. By recognizing the ways in which ideas about time and space reflect and enact broader cultural values, accommodations can be made to prevent frustrations and build respectful working relationships.

Aligning with the Cosmic Order

In the Indian context, the universe, or the macrocosm, looms large in everyday life. The influence of a greater order is woven into the routine activities of an individual. A person functions as a microcosm, a unique mini-universe with its own self-sustaining working structure that is believed to reflect the larger patterns of universal order. Any size organizational unit, including the world, society, family, and even corporate entities are all examples of microcosms. For there to be continued order and harmony in the world or in an individual's life, macrocosm and microcosm need to be kept in alignment. Humans can maintain balance with the macrocosm of the universe by attending to the intersections of time and space.

From the very beginning of the birth of a human life, both the time and place of that birth create a unique relationship between that person and the position of different planetary bodies at that moment. A map, or astrological chart, traces when and where a life begins in relation to the universe. The interpretation of this chart is a horoscope that provides guidelines to both places and times in a person's life that are more likely to be in or out of alignment with supporting different aspects over a lifetime—from favorable finances and career choices to marriages.

It becomes second nature for many people to consult their chart before making major decisions. What would be seen as a suitable match for a job placement, for example, are conditions of location, type of work, and windows of time in a person's life that increase the possibilities for success. The start of a job, as with the beginning point of anything new in a person's life, becomes an especially important time to mark. Hire or start dates for an employee will often only be chosen after a flip through the calendar to make sure the best day

Ingredient 10: Cultural Views of Time and Space

(and sometimes time) aligns with the potential for success and avoids aspects associated with extra difficulty. Things to avoid include certain moon phases, eclipses, or certain days of the week associated with troublesome gods. Depending on which god the individual, family, or business has a relationship, the days of good or bad fortune, marked as auspicious or inauspicious days, may vary.

The most often practiced form of alignment with auspicious time is the temporal window during which the marriage ceremony should take place. For example,

> *Hemkant and Alice meet and fall in love when they join a U.S. software company. When they decide to tie the knot, the first thing Hemkant and his parents plan to do is to consult their family priests for auspicious dates to solemnize their engagement and marriage. Hemkant's parents came to the United States from India and inculcated in him a deep respect for Indian traditions and values. Alice, on the other hand, grew up in South Africa in a very different kind of household. Her scientist Indian father and educationist British mother gave her the legacy of rational thinking and love of freedom. However, Alice admires Hemkant's respect for Indian customs, and his family's wishes, and even joins his parents in choosing auspicious dates with their priest much to the amusement of her parents.*

Everyday operations and timelines of projects can be affected by the same desire to increase potential success through cosmic alignment. Major new projects may not start on a Monday, thus affecting the scheduling of meetings. Launch dates for marketing a product or the grand opening of any new business will also be matched to the best possible day to offset potential obstacles. Barring Saturday, most other days are considered good for ceremonies in general, although a consultation with a trained priest or astrologer can determine dates and times more precisely. There will often be minor shifts in scheduling to accommodate this belief.

Sometimes a big block of time is considered auspicious or inauspicious. For example, the two weeks of *shraadh* that precede the nine-day Navaratri festival that falls within September–October is considered inauspicious. During this time, Hindus often travel to Gaya, Varanasi, and other holy towns to pay homage to their ancestors during this period, pray for their blessings, and in general try to remember the departed. It is advised not to start any new commercial ventures during this time frame. During the ninth month of the Islamic calendar, Muslims observe Ramadan, when they observe a total fast from sunrise to sunset, eating with family and friends after dusk with the *iftar* dinner. Ramadan is the most venerated and blessed month of the Islamic year. Even though most work and life responsibilities continue, due to the discipline and focus on this practice that reprioritizes life toward God and family, it is usually not the best time to engage in important business transactions.

On an annual scale, festivals abound in India that celebrate significant events in the lives of religious founders, gods' birthdays, marriages or victories, as well as communal rituals of remembrance of past events. Religious holidays are another way for people to realign themselves with their relationships to a god(s) by participating in the recreation of a mythological event or sacred history within their families and communities. Multiple religious calendars create a large number of official and unofficial holidays that affect the scheduling of employees, as well as project timelines. Gift giving may be appropriate in certain circumstances, especially for new year's celebrations.

Linear and Cyclical Time

The value of time and how it is interpreted and prioritized differs from culture to culture. Myths about how the world was created reveal factors that influence people's orientation toward time. The religious worldviews that have had the biggest influence on Western notions of time envision the creation of the world as happening once at a singular point in time, and progressing along an orderly number of days (six) with the seventh day one of rest. Judaism, Christianity, and Islam all offer this narrative as an explanation for the beginning of time, and also the basis for the seven-day week. As soon as time begins, it marches continuously forward to its inevitable conclusion at another decisive point marked as the "end of time." For some denominations, this end point is determined by religious events, such as the return of a god, destruction of world orders and/or change into a peaceful one, or judgment by a higher being, to name a few. The world is created once, and a person lives one lifetime.

In other worldviews that have been influential in Indian contexts, both the creation and the destruction of the world have happened many times and in many different ways. Time repeats itself, and keeps going continuously without end. Destruction or chaos is incorporated into time as just one point along a trajectory that eventually repeats itself.

Following from this, a person also lives multiple times through a process of reincarnation. The influence of karma, a belief that actions affect consequences, creates the circumstances that often trigger birth into another lifetime. For many religious traditions, one of the main goals is to stop this karmic based cycle of rebirth completely through modifying behaviors.

A cyclical view of time creates a more fluid or relaxed appearance to time. IST or "Indian Standard (Stretched) Time," is the nickname that describes a sense of timing without regard to attuning actions precisely to a clock. When time repeats and does not hold the weight of one chance, there is no need to rush around to get things done. There will be other opportunities that will come around. The good news is that this instills the possibility for fresh starts and for timing to be more naturally matched to the type of project and creativity needed. At the same time, IST causes some of the worst conflicts between people from different cultures, as people are routinely "late" for meetings and appointments and deadlines are not absolute. Adopting a more flexible attitude toward time will alleviate many frustrations. Even though many people have adjusted their own habits to be more punctual when working with Western clientele, if a task or project needs to be completed, setting an earlier deadline than necessary may be a helpful strategy.

The nine-to-five workday is also not to be found in Indian contexts for many reasons. Looking at a typical workday illustrates priorities that place family time over work, and practicalities that account for weather conditions as well as customer base. In general the workday starts much later to allow for time in the morning to be with families and personal activities. The largest meal of the day is around 2:00 P.M., and many people return home to eat and take rest afterward, during the hottest portion of the day. People in small commercial businesses return to work in the late afternoon/early evening, and stay open later, as many people find it more comfortable to run errands when it cools down.

This pattern adjusts according to industry, city living, and clientele demand. For example, business process outsourcing (BPO) workers for European and American financial institutions match their hours of business to the prevalent time zone of their clients. Workers may have shifts that start at 8:00 P.M. and go into the early morning hours. A typical 24-hour day is often split into three eight-hour shifts to match multiple countries. There is a willingness to shift work hours to bring in more lucrative contracts, as well as to work longer hours. Also, more people commute and do not return home in the middle of the day, modeling more of a continuous workday that both starts later and ends later. As opposed to the government sector, the private sector is much better in discipline, accountability, and punctuality. Surprisingly, public sector undertakings, such as building a world-class mass rapid transit system, or Delhi Metro, has completed many of its projects on or before deadline so far. India's IT and BPO industries blazed new trails through being willing to shift work hours, and other industries have adopted their professional delivery of services and world-class corporate governance.

Gods in the Cubicle: Sanctifying Office Space

In many American contexts, workspaces reflect a person's values and personality. Organized people may have color-coded filing systems with machine printed labels, while others use stack and pile filing methods only understood by its singular user. A few pictures of family, especially a spouse and/or kids is typical, sometimes pets, as well as few other trinkets, are mixed in with any plaques signifying achievement or certificates marking credentials. All of these individual expressions will be circumscribed within the company's public enactment of its business culture, ranging along a spectrum from plain conformity to uninhibited creativity. Depending on the work environment, these individual spaces often are kept relatively free of items marking religious affiliation.

In India, a person's religious background is often a known, public identity due to cultural markers of dress, body markings, and names. Shopkeepers indicate their religion through insignia hanging on the walls—perhaps a clock showing the Ka'ba in Mecca, or hours of operation that reveal what holidays are celebrated or daily religious practices are performed. Business spaces are not completely devoid of religion—all the spaces of a person's life, whether home or office—are touched by religious ways of being to different degrees.

> *Beatrice, manager of the Asian operations of a German firm from Hong Kong, is on a business visit to India. On her way to the Gurgaon office just outside Delhi, she stops at a gift store to buy presents for her Indian colleagues. The store is open but not ready for business since the owner is in the middle of participating in puja. Beatrice observes the owner standing with eyes closed and hands held together in prayer before the images of the gods Lakshmi and Ganesh. The owner's wife puts freshly made jasmine garlands around the necks of the statues*

Ingredient 10: Cultural Views of Time and Space   125

and then raises a decorated plate full of offerings of sweets and light in front of the images. After the ritual is over, the owner applies red paste on his own forehead and offers it to any other people present. Blessed sweets are then passed around. Beatrice is proud of being included in the ceremony and does not erase the red mark from her forehead. She goes on to pick out the few gifts she had forgotten to bring from Hong Kong and heads in to the office.

The routine closing of a shop, whether pausing for Hindu rituals or for daily prayers in Muslim market places, is typically brief and reminds the devoted that business is a blessing from god. If you begin to look around, you may see small signs of divine blessings or protection in office spaces. Before Abhi starts his day, he may log in to make an online offering to pay for a ritual to be done by priests on his behalf to bless his computer, and other "tools" of his profession. Joseph may have a glassine paperweight with a crystallized mirror image of the local form for Mother Mary. Hanging near the copier may be a black string holding a dried out lime, stained red and knotted in to the end,

Puja in the workplace: worship being conducted near computers at the beginning of the stock market year in Mumbai, India.

as a talisman to ward away problems with the new office electronic machines. These markers tend to be subtle, but reminders of the belief in divine presence even in workspaces.

Typically the cubicles or work desks are sparse, low on personalization and people appear to have a low emotional attachment to the space. This is especially true for the majority of workers in government and other public sector jobs where work desks change dynamically and are routinely shared with others. For example, in a bank people work in rotations and constantly move from one desk to another. Privacy and allocated work area security is also a major concern in government jobs. Offices are usually cramped desks in huge hallways overflowing with people and visitors, leaving little room for safety and upkeep of one's personal effects.

Some personal effects may find a place in work cubicles in private corporations where everyone has a designated work area allocated on a long-term basis. In these Indian office spaces, it is not commonplace to find pictures of spouses, kids, or pets. Keeping animals as pets is not that widespread in India in middle-class families; it is more a preserve of the upper middle class or rich strata of society. Some people may keep small wallet-size photographs of their spouse and kids but, in general, they keep family matters private and to a limited circle of close friends. In the same vein, some may like to keep a small statue of god for good luck, but in general Indians do not feel the need to display their religion or gods in their own private workspaces. They always wear it on their sleeves already. You may find people with all kinds of talisman around their neck or colorful strings and bracelets worn on their wrists. The display of religion is more "on" the person, and in their name, rather than on her desk.

At the Center of It All

The floor plans of Hindu temples reveal a template for an arrangement of space that is highly valued and is often imitated in other contexts. By duplicating the spatial clues of a temple within a business or other context, it allows the people within those spaces to signify aspects of authority and relationship.

Temples regularly house many gods, but usually one god will be identified as the primary figure for a particular temple. The principal god resides near the center or center back of the complex, within an enclosed space. The doorway is to the east, so the god can wake up to face the rising sun. In larger temples, there will be a passageway around this main enclosure that people will circumambulate in a clockwise direction. Other gods may be placed within their respective quadrants along this passageway. Sometimes there are multiple passageways that circle around the main god, as well as the development of separate full enclosures to house other gods on a growing temple compound.

When people first enter larger temples, depending on the time they have, they will not go straight to the main god. When they first enter, stepping over the threshold with their right foot, they will turn to the left to start a full clockwise circuit of the temple. The first god placed to the left is usually Ganesh, the elephant-headed god, who is the god of good beginnings and remover of obstacles. The placement of the other gods is dictated by astrological considerations (certain gods are associated with different directions), regional preferences, as well as space constraints and restrictions. Many of the famed Indian temples follow Vaastu principles in their design and architecture, which is the ancient and traditional Indian system of design based on directional alignments. Certain directions and corners of a plot of land, a building, or a room are believed to bring in positive or negative effects. Each directional unit will be beneficial or could pose obstacles toward different types of tasks to be performed in each area. For example, bathrooms and kitchens, or essentially rooms with drains, should not be placed in the financial quadrant as a way to prevent the unintended loss of money, as if it was being flushed down a drain.

In a business context, use of enclosures, centering of authority and reception areas often follow temple patterns and/or Vaastu principles. The highest form of authority in that environment will often be found in a centrally located enclosed space toward the back, rather than a corner office. There will be multiple other people to go through before you can reach the head person. It all depends on that first interaction with the receptionist, who can remove obstacles, or create delays. You may just have to be patient and begin the circuit. Many of the people along the way can be helpful in your requests before you reach the main person. On the way out, there will be others to visit to wrap up loose ends. In this way, spatial arrangements suggest a pattern of behavior to follow.

> *After spending three months searching for a suitable property to house his corporate office, Tony Grant, the President of a European conglomerate,*

is finally a happy man and compliments his Vice President of Administration, Venky Rao, for his efforts. However, after a fortnight into the new office, Tony is surprised to see plans for minor construction to change the arrangement of offices, and to move the pantry to the opposite side of the room. After consulting with a Vaastu expert, Venky explained to Tony that the accounting office needed to be shifted to maximize income, and the reception area should be placed in the northeast to best welcome new business. A mirror was also being placed at the end of the hallway to counteract the directional misalignment in the building. To Tony, these changes did not make much sense, but as the cost was not great, he signs off on the project. He takes a philosophical perspective and decides that if this satisfies his employees and creates a positive work atmosphere, there is no harm in making the changes.

In some places of business, height has replaced centrality to signify authority. A desk or chair may be raised onto a platform for those in supervisory positions. Different kinds of chairs and desks, both in terms of quality, size, and height for different levels of officials and executives are the norm in India in both government and private corporations. Who lives or occupies what floor in a house or building also has significance. In multistory houses with two to three floors, in the past landlords tended to occupy the ground floor, while upper floors were rented out or given to sons and relatives. In the modern era, this idea has shifted: the higher the better is the new motto. Penthouses or the top floor luxury residences that allow freedom to customize living and working spaces according to the status of the owner are newly prized statements of power through height. Similarly, top bosses in multistory buildings occupy the higher floors, much like they do in America, leaving the lower floors for people in intermediary and lower ranked positions.

In general, square or rectangular tables are still the norm, as they signify a barrier and an uneven power differential. The introduction of round tables into shared workspaces is a newer trend that decentralizes hierarchy and invites more participation. The spatial arrangements of an office can tell you how open the business is to group collaboration versus chain of command approaches.

Summary Points

Paying attention to aspects of time and space provide clues that help you to interpret and navigate the culture of a particular business environment. Some things to keep in mind:

Time is flexible. A cyclical view of time helps create a more fluid sense of timing that is not as pressing as in other cultures. Some flexibility is helpful in setting up appointments and deadlines in order to account for IST, or Indian stretchable time.

Workspace is sacred space. For many small businesses as well as office workers, the tools of their work and spaces within which they work fall under an extension of religion. God's blessings help overcome challenges and bring forth prosperity in the workplace. Public displays of such acknowledgment may be part of daily puja by shopkeepers, online pujas, and other material traces in people's personal and shared work environments.

Alignment brings order. Daily, weekly, monthly, and annual calendars all contribute to placing a person and their activities as much in alignment with cosmic factors as possible. Attuning with a higher order to boost the potential for success or avoid unnecessary obstacles mostly affects scheduling.

Spatial clues signify degree of hierarchy. Centrality within an office space, and verticality in desk and chair height, as well as placement of the offices of higher-ranked executives on upper office floors, mimics clues about power found in spatial arrangements in temples.

Chapter 13

Ingredient 11: Women in the Workplace

Women have always been part of the workforce. In villages and cities, women run teashops, heal patients, winnow and sell rice, build and engineer multistoried housing structures, and are elected officials at regional and national levels. There are certain jobs that are still divided along gender lines—very few women drive auto rickshaws or taxis, and yet positions in elementary schools continue to be filled mostly by women. Images of abandoned widows, child marriages, and dowry deaths are confusing when women have also held some of the highest positions in government, including Prime Minister, as well as lead companies as CEOs in media, hospitality, biomedical, and banking industries. Cultural messages about women are complicated and any generalizations about women need to be carefully qualified and contextualized. With this disclaimer in mind, it is helpful to follow the major changes that have occurred over the last decade due to the influx of women into a range of Indian business environments. This chapter focuses especially on cultural assumptions that affect women in business.

Escorted and Independent

In more conservative Indian models of gender roles, women have been escorted and protected by fathers, brothers, husbands, and eventually also grown sons. Women without chaperones are still viewed in some sectors, especially rural areas, as a potential liability to family honor. Even for foreign women traveling solo in India, the desire to understand who is responsible for looking out after her is an important piece of information. It is not unusual to be asked within minutes of meeting new people about marriage status, and if traveling alone, when a husband or father would be joining the woman. While the first question is still asked even in business settings, people are getting more used to the idea of women traveling solo for work.

Even among the urban middle and upper classes, safeguards are instituted to balance out growing freedoms for their daughters with the mindset of guarding against situations that would put both the girl and family into social ostracism. Women's colleges are popular as a way to continue supervision, while giving access to higher education. However not all colleges in India are gender-segregated and businesses certainly are not.

The unchaperoned nature of women entering into working environments has led to mixed messages that are still being socially and legally sorted out. Some of this has to do with the redefinition of appropriate places for women to be and what governs interactions in those new spaces. To date, there are not many systems put into place to address inappropriate behavior toward women from colleagues or supervisors. In part, this is due to being in the process of figuring out how to create systems that can effectively replace the role that families played in proactively preventing problems, as well as educating new mindsets that women in increasingly independent situations do not automatically equate with the potential for social disgrace or the transfer of awkward power differentials.

In this process of transition, several strategies have been adopted. The first involves a chaperone replacement of sorts, or at least the inclusion of a male figurehead. In family run businesses, there is less of a problem. Women who work within the family business do so under the larger protection of an extension of family dynamics already in place. Increasingly, businesses are developed independently outside of the family support structure by people from different levels of society, as well as foreigners. Alecca, a fashion designer based in India since 2006, notes the strategy of employing an Indian male business partner, even though it does not resolve all challenges:

> Being a woman cannot help anyone here in India. It is a huge challenge, especially in my field where all workers are men! Well, I have an Indian male partner who runs operations for me. I would have never been able to start up the business as a foreign woman. From purchases to dealing with staff, it is all a challenge. You have to count your fingers every time you hand out money! Any transaction is at risk of becoming corrupt, from the smallest eight rupee purchase, to the biggest of course. What makes me

feel better is to know that even my male Indian partner gets taken to the cleaners once in a while...so I don't take it personally![1]

Having a male business partner or colleague can go a long way to facilitate transactions, to help with negotiations, and just bypass a lot of unnecessary questions. What this does is effectively give the appearance of a family dynamic, even if in actuality the woman is in charge. While this may be an unnecessary strategy in many situations, or may seem anachronistic, the path of least resistance may be a good option in some cases.

A second option that some companies have developed is to create a "family feeling" within an organization that has an effect on office procedures and etiquette. One notable example of this involves a situation that arises out of the odd hours the call centers and business process outsourcing (BPO) offices require, in order to be online with operating hours in Europe and America. Many young men and women are working in the middle of the night and need to go to work or return safely home between 1:00 and 4:00 A.M. In order to assuage family concerns, company policies may be extended to address problems regarding late hours. For example, one female data analyst notes, "Fortunately for me, this has never been an issue but I know a lot of my colleagues in other teams have issues like this. Indians in general start their day late and end late. In quite a few companies these days, the companies arrange for cab drops at night, but I know this is not a policy everywhere."[2]

Companies that have built factories and headquarters outside of city limits have become vigilant about vetting a staff of drivers that will prevent inappropriate harassment by bringing them into the company "family," with varying degrees of success. In general, this is only one of the many issues that arise within office interactions, as both men and women work in close quarters with each other. For many men, this may be the first time that they work extended hours with nonfamily females.

Gender Dynamics

In a 2005 collection of interviews with 21 female leaders of India, many interviewees maintained no experience of gender bias over the course of their careers at the top of their companies. According to others, such as Ekta Kapoor, a leading figure in the TV industry, a "slim degree of male domination and gender bias does persist," even though the focus should be on the quality of work regardless of gender.³ A common thread among the interviews with women in the upper echelons of the banking industry in particular, demonstrate an emphasis on fair hiring and promotion practices. Lalita D. Gupte, joint managing director of ICICI bank, notes:

> ICICI Bank is an organization driven by meritocracy. We view merit and performance as the core criteria for promotions; they are the rationale behind the underlying success of several young professionals in our organization. Gender and background have no role to play in this regard. Contoured by a sensitive and uplifting spirit that lies within its façade, ICICI had been neutral to both males and females alike, in its treatment of employees over its time frame of fifty years.⁴

Similarly, Naina Lal Kidwai, deputy chief executive officer of HSBC, emphasizes a necessary awareness of company policies and practices:

> Besides keeping a watchful eye on how many women we hire, we need to actively monitor the percentage of women who get in and the percentage that continues to stay. To make certain they continue to stay, it is mandatory on our part to see that we don't make exceptions or create a community of favours. The core essence merely lies in being fair and just—with an eye on yourself, of course [*sic*].⁵

In alignment with Gupte and Kidwai's remarks, corporations such as ICICI and HSBC that have a higher percentage of women employed within the higher levels of management tend to be more conscious of instituting gender equality in the workplace.

At the same time, some of the women leaders also indicated past struggles that have been overcome in some cases, but also continue to be a major issue among lower levels of management and the workforce. Sulajja Firodia Motwani, joint managing Director of Kinetic Engineering, points to the rapid social evolution in gender roles as a contributor to harassment. As she notes,

> A few generations ago, women fought for their basic right to vote. They went through the stage of being restricted to their homes. Those were the days when women's liberation was a myth, in spite of all that was being said about it. Then came the

backlash. Sexual harassment grew rampant at the workplace. To begin with, women were not treated professionally; they weren't accepted as professional colleagues quite so easily.[6]

Tarjani Vakil, the first Indian woman to head a bank and financial institution, remembers the situation well when she joined IDBI in 1965. She was the only woman among 30 hired colleagues that year. As her interviewers M. Amarnath and D. Ghosh note, "Though Tarjani performed exceedingly well in her career, her gender stood in the way of the training that she needed. Quite protective of her, seniors didn't send her abroad for training programmes [sic] since they believed it was impossible for a woman to travel abroad all by herself and were worried about how she would manage were they to send her alone. Over the entire span of her 17-year career, she was sent for training only for ten days." Vakil believes that this protective approach was due to there not being many career women at the time. In addition to missed training opportunities, it also meant that she had to struggle to win the right to be sent on factory inspections and other job tasks either because there were many male workers on the premise, or her seniors did not want her to go alone.[7]

According to Naina Lal Kidwai, the reason that many more women hold higher positions in the banking industry today may be due, in part, to location. As she states, "I feel the work environment is substantially more encouraging in the banking sector." Moreover, most banks are located in metros. Consequently, one doesn't have to travel much. Furthermore, for women it is easier to interact with educated and qualified men. Banking is a far cry from a marketing career or a job that warrants heavy traveling across the country.[8] While the banking industry is clearly in the lead in terms of gender dynamics, many other industries are following suit, utilizing any advantages that keep women professionals on the job, and working through each challenge that may arise.

Harassment

Sexual harassment, called "eve-teasing" in India, may be illegal, but the definitions of forms of harassment and legal burden of proof are not developed to the same extent as in the United States. In 1997, the Supreme Court in India first defined sexual harassment and acknowledged it as a form of gender discrimination, providing the Vishaka guidelines for the implementation of clear policies, preventative measures, and grievance procedures in the workplace. Compliance is hard to track, enforcement has been minimal, and legislative bills, such as the 2007 Protection of Women against Sexual Harassment at Workplace Bill (still under deliberation in 2010) have faltered despite repeated efforts on the part of several organizations, including the National Commission for Women.[9]

In addition to weakened legal avenues, the more pervasive obstacle is that the shame of unwanted advances leads to a culture of silence. Women do not want to say anything, because in general it is assumed that it was their behavior, dress, or in general "unchaperoned state" that invited the harassment. One single young Indian woman in her late-20s, Savitri, spoke candidly about sexual harassment at the workplace:

> I think a lot of women in India go through this and I am not an exception. Sadly, most of us don't even speak up which means most of these men get away with whatever it is they are doing! It is more like a social stigma thing. Since such things until recently, were never publicly discussed in India, we think a million times before we use official channels to get out of this mess.[10]

While Indian women experience harassment, foreign women are also working against stereotypes, as well as being unaware of how their behavior is perceived within Indian cultural models. Access to American films and availability of Internet sources contributes to a narrow view of foreign women. As Greek designer Alecca notes, "Indian men are very attracted by white 'Gori' women. They have this notion that we are easy to get women and that we have no 'culture and tradition' just because we don't look down when they talk to us! So, that is a problem we face on a daily basis... but it quickly gets sorted out when we make things clear, though it is unavoidable!"[11]

Gabriela, who heads a branch of an MNC working in the provision of infrastructure services to municipalities, observes the importance of context:

> Strangely enough, the fact that I am a woman seems to have been less a problem in India than in France. In India I feel I am seen first as a foreigner, gender comes second. Mind you, I am working with 2 major types of people: the "Babus" and local engineers (never had any problems), and the Indian private partners that we develop business with. I had once a problem with the second

category, since the person took kind friendship for a very wrong signal. But after refocusing and putting limits, the guy got the message and the relationship went on clear grounds.[12]

The way business is done in India lends itself to a blurring of personal and business spaces that invites more familiar interactions, especially through the emphasis on hospitality. Gabriela continues:

> The problem I feel in India is that when you are the boss and you interact with other bosses, there is hardly no limit between the professional sphere and the private sphere, therefore I am invited to all those private parties, I get to know the family, and rapidly, some kind of proximity develops. And as a woman, some Indian men can just get the wrong signals, so one should be aware of this and adapt to its attitude.[13]

Many of the women interviewed for this chapter offer several pieces of advice for other women. In general, the main message is to be proactive when possible. Gabriela suggests an emphasis on professionalism, "[N]ever allow any one to go 'over the board,' even if it is a joke. Furthermore, I would advise not to get dressed in an improper way, and in case any one gets beyond tolerable limits in the professional space, try to refocus the interaction on exclusively professional grounds, and be extremely clear and firm on what is acceptable and what is not."[14]

When Savitri was sent to the United States for a six-month training period, she noted that most men she encountered at work whether in India or abroad were "very well-mannered and decent." Her advice centered on avoiding physical contact (arms placed over her shoulder, hugs), as well as being aware that flirting and casual dating are not common interactions for Indian women, and especially might be misconstrued in a workplace. While American companies have a range of policies on workplace relationships, in India, companies are particularly sensitive to avoiding any appearance of inappropriate interactions among its mixing of employees in order to maintain a good reputation. From a particular incident Savitri encountered, she suggests the following, "Avoid touching apart from a casual handshake once in a while. I know when I was in the U.S., as I was leaving the place, I went to take a pic[ture] with one of the managers there and he put his arm around me (he was rather old and very fatherly). But I am not sure how well that will go down with most other women."[15]

In general, while India works out more clearly defined harassment policies and laws, it is a good idea to be mindful of behavior that may be misread within the cultural context of gendered behavior patterns within India. This may appear sexist, but right now it continues to be a reality that businesspeople of either gender need to be aware of when working in India. American body language tends to be more open, but what is acceptable and "friendly" in one place, can be misread in other contexts.

Women in Leadership

Women who rise through the ranks, such as former (late) Prime Minister Indira Gandhi, are often associated with goddesses who protect the country, drawing authority from the imagery of the many-armed Durga for example. Many of the descriptions of women in positions of power highlight qualities of strength. Ravina Raj Kohli, former President of STAR news, is described as a "tough, iron-willed lady who says 'No!' to nothing and concocts a wonderful creation from zilch. She has always been happy in places that have granted her complete authority and independence."[16] At the forefront of the fashion industry, Ritu Kumar emphasizes the women-warrior model when she states, "Women today are more advanced than they were ten years ago. Over a span of the next ten years, I foresee an explosion of women in all sectors. Men-folk should brace themselves for a real tough fight from their female colleagues."[17] According to Kumar's interviewees, "Not the slightest fear or hesitation in Ritu's mind has ever held her back from her goal."[18]

One of the outstanding sources of that strength, along with other qualities that many Indian women feel make them good leaders and managers, is identified from within their own domestic experiences, as mothers and sometimes members of joint family households. The managing director of Apollo Hospitals, Preetha Reddy, specifically points to this system as a training ground for management: "The joint family system, predominant in earlier times, have trained women to live harmoniously with cousins, aunts, and uncles, increasing their adjustability and flexibility. Indian women are consequently much more capable of managing people effectively and coping with workplace and career-related stressors than women in other parts of the world."[19] Shahnaz Hussein, CEO of Shahnaz Herbals, adds, "As a woman efficiently juggles her roles as wife, mother, homemaker and career woman, she acquires the values of patience, time-management and budget handling."[20] These qualities lead to the "strong-willed" model of the matriarch that transfers well between home and professional spheres.

At the same time, while business women in middle or upper management or executive levels have the advantage of an appeal to divine authority or strong family matriarchs, other messages of men being lords and protectors of women still exist to different degrees. Mostly there seems to be a gap between women in the highest levels of power who insist "gender bias is being dispensed with,"[21] and those at other rungs that still indicate difficulties. As Savitri, who regularly takes on supervisory duties in Bangalore mentions, "For women in the managerial position, men find it very difficult to take orders from them!"[22] The model does not always trickle down to lower levels, and there are still vast discrepancies in certain industries in terms of division of labor. In an analysis of the overall gender structure in back office services, women predominate at what are the more routine (requiring only basic skills) and discretionary (requiring technical training and problem solving) levels of service. Examples include hotel reservations, order taking, data verification, claims processing, and remote secretarial assistance. Men are more likely to be hired at the specialized level (requiring specific expertise and managerial authority), with tasks that include dispute resolution, accounting, Web site management, medical records management, technical online support, and publishing work in indexing, abstracts, research, and technical writing.[23] This gender discrepancy in skill-level opportunities suggests further research needs to be done to find strategies to lessen this gap.

The call center worker represents a common case example that highlights several important demographic features. Usually in her 20s, college educated, and single, she will typically leave her job upon marriage or to pursue graduate studies that will enable further promotion or other job prospects. While working, this young woman may be the highest earner in the family, often giving over much of her paycheck to support the household expenses of parents and educational and marriage expenses of siblings. This earner status tends to create more freedoms, some financial, others more social in terms of having more self-choice in marriage partners. The trend in this rising middle-class sector is a delay in marriage, and once married, often a further delay in having children—what is often referred to as DINK—double income, no kids.

Part of the challenge of these changes to the social structure is the need for systems to support women who want to work and have a family. Some women indicate the value of the joint family system in providing extended childcare though aunts, sister-in-laws, and so on. Chanda Kocchar, managing director and CEO of ICICI Bank, maintains, "A resource of Indian ethnicity, the joint family culture serves as a backbone and an additional support system to help women tackle their domestic responsibilities—one which women from other corners of the world cannot readily avail of."[24] As many married couples move away from joint families for work opportunities, it has been suggested to larger companies to implement onsite childcare services to encourage the continuation of employment after marriage.[25] As Lalita Gupte notes, practices to support working women have not gone far enough as of yet:

> Women work enthusiastically soon after they graduate from B[usiness]-schools or complete their education in other disciplines. Once married though, they don't get adequate support to help them unearth the right balance between their homes and careers. They need to find the right people to whom they can entrust the responsibility of looking after their children. Organizations must pitch in to help women by granting extended leave to new mothers and introducing flexi-time options for them.[26]

Underlying all of this has to be family support for the woman's career—an attitude that has been undergoing recent changes. Motwani observes, "There has also been an attitudinal change in the mindsets of men who are fresh college graduates; they express a desire to marry financially, economically and emotionally independent women with broad horizons, sharp intellects and minds of their own. Men have begun to respect women whose interests lie in non-domestic activities as well.... We can discern a great difference in the India that we live in as this change has percolated to cities, countrywide."[27]

The landscape of women professionals is changing rapidly, and hopefully with continued awareness and support, women will continue to occupy more positions of leadership.

Themes and New Directions

This chapter has offered several pieces to keep in mind when evaluating gender dynamics that may be influencing the business environments you may find yourself working within. It may be especially difficult to reconcile what appears to be conflicting information. Strong-willed women are found alongside those who may employ a male business partner to deal with negotiations. Some experience little gender bias while others encounter harassment on a regular basis and glass ceilings. There are career women living in joint families, some as the sole or primary earner in the house, and others as part of a DINK couple, living in separate households at times.

The common themes are context and culture. The context determines the likely gender models that may or may not be bearing on the people with which you work. Cultural literacy in India involves knowing some of the various possible factors, including gender, which may surface in interactions with your business partners or team members. Depending on your gender, the gender of those you work with, and in what contexts, attention to gender dynamics will have varying degrees of relevance. Being aware of how one's own behavior may come across and being sensitive to cultural norms are key.

Current research that will help bridge an understanding of how to navigate the intersection of gender and culture is being done by Stacy Blake-Beard, Associate Professor in the School of Management at Simmons College. While teaching in Hyderabad in 2009, she undertook a study focused on mentoring across cultures. She notes that for women from India, there tends to be clear divisions between work and home, with the expectation of being home to raise children. "Also," as Blake-Beard writes, "the societal expectation that cross-gender relationships at work should be tightly constrained meant that behaviors necessary to maintain mentoring relationships (close contact, frequent communication, a measure of vulnerability and sharing) placed these women outside of accepted norms. As a result, they were subject to additional scrutiny and even attacks on their personal character."[28] These observations influence not only mentoring practices, but also many of the expected working relationships encountered in newer American-influenced work settings. Research and the strategies that develop out of the work of consultants and scholars like Blake-Beard offer new directions for attracting and retaining women in positions of leadership in the workplace.

This chapter provides the beginning of an overview of many of the gender dynamics you may encounter, as well as some pointers that are a good start to traversing some of the gendered components of Indian culture.

Summary Points

Indian culture provides a range of gender role models. From family roles as daughters and wives to business and government roles as CEOs and Prime Ministers, women have a variety of access to levels of power, control of resources, and authority-creating strategies that must be determined according to each situation.

Family-based corporate strategies and policies resolve issues of "unchaperoned" women. In some cases, the workplace is being redefined as an extension of family space, among other strategies for creating appropriate spaces for women to inhabit. Clear guidelines for gender interactions continue to reflect struggles to define shifting gender roles.

Body language can easily be misinterpreted across cultures. Be aware of physical interactions and err on the conservative side. Maintain personal boundaries among business colleagues, whether in private or public contexts.

Women experience different levels of gender bias. In different industries and levels of management and employment, there is a wide range of experiences of discrimination and harassment. While there are tenuous legal guidelines in place to prevent problems and redress complaints, on the practical level, much more work needs to be done to support compliance.

Cultural models from the domestic sphere foster excellent management qualities, including, time management, flexibility, multitasking, and patience. Many women in India draw upon domestic skills as a resource in their working environments. This is instead of feeling that work and family are incompatible pursuits.

Chapter 14

Seasoned to Perfection, or How to Mix Your Ingredients with Success

It is important to remember that Indian customers are not a concept, they are living people. Indians are full of paradoxes and contradictions. They do not fit into any existing model customer profiles. They demand a serious analysis of their aspirations and wants in the context of their income levels and they always want good value for their money. These psychographic traits get compounded manifold by a long history of social traditions and cultural predilections.

Culture is a complex set of human attitudes, preferences, expectations, and behavioral norms that people innately learn from their families and communities within a geographical area or region. Within each larger culture, there are multiple, overlapping subcultures with which one needs to be aware. But in starting with the larger culture, as we present in this book, a serious and careful approach goes a long way to making inroads toward understanding, empathizing, and finding some common ground to make a good start. With time and extended exposure, you will be able to immerse yourself in unearthing the deeper nuances behind behavior and communication patterns in each context. At first, it takes patience and perseverance to decode these intangibles, but this task is central to the process of gaining trust, loyalty, and respect. Well-known Polish reporter Ryszard Kapuscinski states it well when he writes in his *Travels with Herodotus*, "I realized then what now seems obvious: a culture would not reveal its mysteries to me at a mere wave of my hand; one has to prepare oneself thoroughly and at length for such an encounter."[1]

Let's begin by examining what happens when you end up offending the cultural sensibilities of your business partners in spite of your best intentions. As Virginia Valentine, founder of Semiotic Solutions, asserts, "Culture isn't inert. It's pretty ert. If it isn't working for you, then it is probably working against you."[2]

Business Case: Texacon's Missing Anchors

A Houston based U.S. engineering company, Texacon Technologies Incorporated, tentatively selects Anchor Engineering Ltd, Chennai, for a joint venture partnership. Texacon's finance director, William Kenney, arrives in India to do the groundwork but finds heat, humidity, and air pollution very unsettling. The food is too spicy and hot for him, while traffic snarls and road jams annoy him to his wit's end. He loves the attention and hospitality, but feels uneasy with formality, hierarchy, and his colleagues' casual attitude toward time. Feeling awkward with being addressed as "Mr. Kenney," he tells them to call him Bill while trying to be friendly and on a first name basis with everyone. When Anchor's managers shake their heads from side to side during a meeting, Bill interprets that as disagreement, calls up Houston, and makes some changes, which in turn puzzles his Indian colleagues. He grumbles when an Anchor VP asks for more time to study project details before signing and routinely barges into CEO G. Venkatesh Swamy's office to share his frustrations.

From the perspective of the Anchor managers, they see Bill's behavior as disrespectful, which brings in palpable tension and discomfort in their interactions. Negotiations hit a wall and even settled agreements become a moot point as his Indian partners feel slighted and seriously undermined. Bill's aggressive stance and his obsession with completing the deal make him appear rude and impolite for being unwilling to examine the finer details of agreements that will lay the foundation for a more enduring partnership. Bill does not look like a guy they can trust and do business with.

On the other hand, Bill also gets suspicious of Anchor's abilities to meet Texacon's stringent quality standards and time management requirements. He feels that Indian managers, though technically brilliant and very capable, are timid, casual, and even unprofessional due to not speaking their mind and appearing to be servile to their bosses. He finds their attitude toward time and punctuality very frustrating. Bill reaches the conclusion that Texacon and Anchor are not compatible, suspends deliberations, and takes an earlier flight back home.

So, what goes wrong? Having started out as an honored guest and colleague, Bill ends up unworthy of the trust and confidence of his Indian colleagues. A number of missteps and unintentional actions punctuate Bill's interaction with his hosts, as cultural illiteracy leads him to commit one faux pas after another. That's the trap you may find yourself in when working with people from another culture. Our culture(s) color the view of the world we live in and influence the way we interact and develop relationships with others. Understanding culture and adapting accordingly is essential to success in business. Gestalt psychology, a theory of mind and brain, opines that we see things as we are, not as things are. This is even more apparent when we operate in an unfamiliar culture. The potential for cultural miscommunication has serious consequences, as this example with Bill highlights. Fortunately, many problems can be avoided with more attention to culture, as the rest of the case studies in this chapter demonstrate.

India's Formidable IT Sector

It is worthwhile to observe how well-understood and well-timed cultural information has played a part in shaping India as the leading IT and business process outsourcing destination of the world. The first movers in the IT field enjoyed certain inherent advantages:

- Infosys, Wipro, Tata Consultancy Services, and so on had been doing business with the United States preceding the arrival of broadband Internet in the late 1990s that opened up partnership opportunities. They used their knowledge of U.S. corporate culture to adapt their companies accordingly.
- Many engineers and programmers had worked in the United States on Y2K projects, which gave them a unique comfort level and facilitated communication between teams.
- IT companies set up informal work environments, aligning themselves with an American business model since most of the clients were from the United States.
- Work ethic in these companies was very strict, high on discipline and conformity, but very dynamic and exciting, which suited the task-oriented mindset of Indians.

The above set of benefits gave leading IT companies an immense edge. Such advantages also worked favorably in consulting industries to a large extent. Taking pointers from Indian IT companies on how they adapted and retooled their organizational structures, management systems, and resources planning to service their clients in the United States and Europe, American giants like GE, IBM, Accenture, and Cisco set in motion their own custom fit modifications to work synergistically with their Indian partners. Since the IT industry was relatively new in India, there was little management baggage and time hardened corporate habits for them to cope with. These companies were already operating in India for a good number of years and were familiar with Indian culture and corporate behavior. The playing field from both sides was thus nearly leveled for both U.S. and Indian IT companies. Some other adjustments made by the U.S. companies were as follows:

- To neutralize competition from their Indian counterparts and to take advantage of the abundant availability of technology savvy talent at competitive costs, the American companies hired Indians in large numbers.
- Some U.S. companies like IBM and Hewlett Packard also acquired locally grown technology companies to increase their manpower strength in addition to recruiting local talent.
- To deal with Indians' casual attitude toward punctuality and time management, the corporations provided company vehicles to pick up and drop off employees from home.
- They instituted the best HR practices, such as investing in training, health care, and benefits, besides paying well. They genuinely valued their employees in a way that in turn ensured retention and minimized turnover, and at the same time helped them engage in practices that reciprocated Indian hospitality.
- Project deliverables were structured in tangible and quantifiable terms to deal with the issue of ambiguity in Indian culture; tasks and performance expectations in contracts and SLA agreements were set in clear, unambiguous terms.

Several companies in other industries that developed an India-centric approach to doing business (i.e., they adapted to its cultural sensitivities) also witnessed success and established a strong presence and market share for their products. Let us examine some of these models and their approach to doing business in India.

McDonald's

McDonald's entered India in 1996 and now operates in many Indian cities. But McDonald's did many firsts in India that they never did anywhere else in the world in their five decade long business history.

Seasoned to Perfection 147

It endeared itself by showing sensitivity and respect toward Indian culture and its religious diversity. Market research indicated that many Hindus do not eat beef and Muslims shun pork, in both cases for religious reasons. It was a big problem for a company that prides itself on its hamburgers and cheeseburgers they have sold in the billions.

But McDonald's looked at the Indian market as a challenge as well as a big opportunity. They had to innovate while maintaining their invaluable brand value and image. So, instead of serving their famed Big Mac to Indians, McDonald's decided to stay away from beef and pork altogether and build a customized vegetarian menu consisting of locally popular ingredients from scratch that they serve with their chicken meals and French fries. They use only vegetable oil for cooking in India, unlike in other markets where they use animal fat for frying. They also keep their vegetarian and nonvegetarian meals totally separate in the entire production chain out of respect to vegetarian customers.

These changes had many benefits. It helped McDonald's not only appear culturally sensitive, but also expanded their reach to a large number of vegetarian Indian populations. Many of McDonald's vegetarian products developed for India are now extremely popular in several overseas markets. McDonald's decision to enter the Indian market through joint ventures with local partners was also a smart move. By building a local supply chain from the ground up in partnership with hundreds of farmers, entrepreneurs, and suppliers, McDonald's was able to cope better with market sensitivities and cultural preferences.[3]

Which of the cultural ingredients described in this book did McDonald's use to script a success story in India?

- Hospitality: Food is central to the notion of hospitality in India and the host's aim is to please the guest(s) without fault. Sacrifice translates into giving primacy to the guest even at the cost of discomfort or loss. McDonald's did both and portrayed itself as good and caring hosts by revamping its menu.
- Dharma of Mission: McDonald's recognized that its sensitivity toward Indian customers' food preferences needed to be incorporated into its overall guiding principles. Marketing and production strategies were shifted to match this new culturally determined aspect.
- Project Process: McDonald's can be credited with setting up its intent very clearly, followed by extensive preparation, and almost a five year long journey with rest points to recharge and

incorporate course corrections as they learnt more about the market and the customers.
- Risk and Action: McDonald's acted in the interest of the greatest number and took a challenging and untried path without knowing whether it would be successful or not.
- Negotiations: McDonald's followed many of Gandhi's ahimsa principles by looking for a market positioning focused on sustainable relationship and long-term payoffs free from the constraints of timeliness and quick returns.

Suzuki Motors

In the early 1980s, Suzuki entered India through a joint venture with a public sector company, Maruti Udyog Limited, to manufacture small fuel-efficient cars for the Indian market, and sell them at a price below the local gas guzzlers, Ambassador and Premium. The car, the Suzuki Maruti 800, became an instant hit. Since its launch, Suzuki has been the market leader in India with an expanding product portfolio and still controls more than 50 percent of the market even after the entry of several international players since economic liberalization in 1991, including Ford, GM, Toyota, Nissan, Samsung, and others.

The leadership of Suzuki has been built on its "value for money" proposition that cuts across customer segments based on its reliable performance, excellent customer service, affordable price, and fuel efficiency. Suzuki started a relationship with the Indian government as an equity sharing arrangement, and implemented a hybrid model of management leadership by enlisting an Indian executive as the chairman. Their business plan committed to the partnership on a long-term basis by building a nationwide network of sales and service outlets. The company also developed a high percentage of indigenization through constructing local ancillary units for parts and equipments. Suzuki improvised and innovated to establish a nurturing relationship with their partners and growing base of local customers. Some of the ingredients that helped them culturally align their business model in India can be identified as:

- Hospitality: Suzuki showed remarkable trust and investment in its partner and reciprocated by ushering in an automotive technology revolution in the country.
- Dharma: Suzuki's mission of dharma went beyond profits and market shares, as shown by investments in manufacturing, R&D,

and ancillary units—all of which created an infrastructure that has helped India emerge as an important hub for the automobile industry.
- Hierarchy: Suzuki recognized the value of hierarchy by accepting a hybrid model of management through welcoming an Indian bureaucrat as its chairman. This model of management structure and control in which Indian government had major equity and Suzuki was a minor partner shielded it against competitors' unfair moves and provided a level playing field allowing it to surge ahead on the strengths of better technology and competitive products.
- Risk and Action: Suzuki used karma yoga principles 3 and 6, by seeking the advice of trusted advisors, in particular senior government officials, and customizing its products for a large number of Indian customers with limited or low income.
- Contract: Suzuki lived up to the spirit of long-term orientation in Indian culture by indigenizing its production to the extent that today India is its main export hub. Suzuki practically laid the foundation of ancillary units for the automotive industry in India, and fulfilled part of its deal by joining hands with local manufacturers and demanding stringent standards.
- Negotiations: Suzuki followed ahimsa principles of equality and respect in establishing its manufacturing and marketing network in India. Many ancillary units, which are multimillion dollar companies today, were small operations that started as proud first time suppliers to a world-renowned company. When labor unrest erupted and accusations of exploitation surfaced, most notably in 2000–2001, Suzuki was challenged to revisit labor policies and consciously remember the people involved in their production processes.[4]

Nokia

In 1995, when cell phones were launched in India, all major handset companies worldwide started jockeying for market shares and leadership position in the virgin industry. Initially prices remained high since airtime was very expensive, keeping the sales volumes quite low. Later, with reduction in airtime prices, launch of prepaid calling cards, and the suspension of incoming call charges, cell phone sales exploded. Today India along with China is one of the fastest growing markets for cell phones in the world. The first mobile call took place on a Nokia handset on a Nokia supported communications network when India introduced cellular telephony in 1995. Nokia, one of the early entrants that bet high stakes on India, is the market leader (>50%) because of its smart innovation in design and price bands, and its endearing adaptability and ever increasing indigenization of manufacturing and services. Early on it designed sturdy handsets for the Indian market that would not fall apart upon hitting the ground and had long battery life to avoid frequent recharging. They marketed single piece compact console units with built-in antenna and stayed away from flip phones and models with pull up antenna units that could easily break. In 1997–1998 Nokia launched 5510, a model that accounted for nearly half of its total handset revenue because of its reliability, sturdiness, and user-friendliness.

Nokia's attention to the potential for a range of customers led them to market a matching variety of handsets from high-end fancy models for the ultra rich to a stripped down basic functional model for low-income groups. Later in 2004, Nokia launched slip-free handsets to beat the sweaty summer with dust covers and even a flashlight, a ready companion during frequent power cuts. The company developed software to support many regional languages and ring tones. Nokia's long-term commitment to India is reflected by its heavy investment in manufacturing units, a national network of distributors and retailers, and employment of a largely Indian workforce to deliver its products and services.[5] Nokia's dominant presence in the Indian cell phone market can be attributed to several cultural ingredients discussed in earlier chapters:

- Hospitality: In return for India's hospitality, Nokia took seriously the specific needs of Indian clientele and developed a range of products and services that focused on pleasing and delighting them. It can be argued that any good business strategy would attempt to do this, but the framework of hospitality that Nokia engaged in gave them a greater edge over other companies that suffered losses and even had to withdraw from the market.
- Dharma of Mission: Nokia espoused its dharma of mission by going above and beyond its duty of selling its products to Indian customers. By designing sturdy handsets equipped with dust covers and flashlights, it showed the company was paying attention to details that mattered. These actions worked wonders for acceptance, visibility, and loyalty of their brands.
- Risk and Action: Price performance is an important matrix for success in the Indian market. Nokia launched a wide range of handsets to service its customers spanning a range of income levels

with competitive price offers. Accessibility of phone service to a greater number of people has facilitated better entrepreneurial support across the board.
- Contract: Nokia built its formidable presence in the country by adhering to a long-term commitment. From the start, Nokia invested in local manufacturing, product design, software development, and other important business components.
- Negotiations: Nokia introduced itself as a caring and respectful corporation, mindful of local customs. The company set up its sales and servicing network by entering into long term relationship with over 200,000 outlets that enlist small local entrepreneurs as business partners and franchisees.[6]
- Project Process: Nokia initially focused on the handset business and then they applied their learning to expand into other allied services, such as network management.

Canon

Canon, Inc. sold its products through distributors until 1997, when it established its 100 percent Indian subsidiary. Generally Indian distributors are not professionally trained and are found lacking in customer relationship management. They tend to prefer their own profits and other short-term gains over the interests of their customers. Canon's story was no different, and there were hundreds of customers who had been victims of unfair practices at the hands of its distributors. For Canon, the road ahead was rough and full of challenges. A lot of ruffled feathers and dormant anger had to be pacified with honest intentions and gentle care.

Canon started by opening several sales offices to sell a limited line of products under the leadership of a senior British Canon executive from London, who was well-versed in Indian culture. He wanted to tread with caution, without repeating the mistakes of the past. Canon put together a management team largely consisting of Indian managers, who brought composite knowledge of the customers and marketplace to the table. The company demonstrated its new long-term commitment to its customers by following the motto—we won't sell if we are not able to service. As it built its sales and service network, Canon spread its presence by appointing dealers nationwide and introduced new India-specific products and services. Gradually, on the strengths of its premium quality products accompanied by world-class customer service, Canon was able to win back the confidence and trust of Indian customers. The outcome of these changes directly translated into increased market share and brand visibility. Today, Canon enjoys leadership positions in several of its product categories and is augmenting its products and services portfolio through new launches and customer engagements.

- Hospitality: Canon's earlier stint in India was murky and its reputation bruised by unprofessional distributors. When it established its 100 percent subsidiary, it based its actions on reciprocity when it decided to postpone establishing a dealer network until it was able to service its customers.
- Dharma of Mission: Canon recognized its dharma of mission by putting the customer at the center of its business plans. It even launched its Indian operations under the leadership of a non-Japanese executive, who was more familiar with Indian culture and business practices.
- Risk and Action: From time to time Canon adhered to all the principles of karma yoga in its business, from owning up to its mistakes, to hiring local talent and even developing low-price products specially designed for the greatest number of people in India.
- Project Process: Canon started small in India. It worked on establishing its credentials and winning the trust of Indian customers before adding new categories of products and venturing into other businesses.
- Contract: Investments in local manufacturing and software development demonstrated its alignment with its long-term commitment to India.
- Leadership: The CEO set a vision in alignment with the advice and work of his colleagues, and then delegated the responsibility of building up various divisions according to local leadership.

In summary, a sound knowledge of India's cultural practices is necessary for any trade or business venture within the country. The case studies discussed and analyzed in this chapter according to the main ingredients of this book demonstrate respect for India, and create an appetizing environment that invites successful interactions with business partners and prospective clients. By taking note of these productive business models, the opportunities to succeed are limitless as you improvise and innovate using your newfound cultural knowledge to adapt in any business context with which you find yourself engaged in India. The sky's the limit!

Conclusion

There are a lot of books on the market about India that all have a particular audience and aim in mind. If you are preparing for a trip to India for business, and want something new to give you an advantage—you have chosen this book wisely! Culture is often the last on people's mind when getting ready to work with clients, teams, and potential partners in other countries. We argue that it should be at the top of the list of priorities. Without cultural literacy of the contexts in which you will be doing business, all the other tools and skills you have as a businessperson, whether fresh out of your MBA program or a seasoned veteran, will not necessarily work in the same way. The great thing about valuing cultural knowledge is that it creates respect and goodwill toward you and your goals the minute you meet your colleagues in India. The more time you invest in it, the more you will be able to adapt to any situation to maximize your results.

We suggest working with the ingredients in several ways no matter where you rank your current level of cultural literacy. A business traveler, like a good master chef, needs to always return to the basics, even when he goes on to learn more advanced dishes. In order to know those ingredients inside and out, she engages all of her senses to absorb their properties, qualities, and any contraindications when mixed or what happens when heat or cold are applied. Our own version of cultural ingredients borrows from this approach. In our analogy, we propose the following strategy:

> **Observe:** Take a look around you. By learning about another culture, it reflects back on your own cultural norms and assumptions. How do you engage in forms of hospitality? What forms of hierarchy do you participate in? Do you have any relationships based on verbal contracts or use intermediaries? By becoming

aware of your own interactions with others, you will better be able to recognize and identify how the ingredients we discuss in this book are at work in Indian business contexts.

Taste: As you get better at identifying the ingredients that are factors in particular situations you find yourself in, you will begin to adapt your approach to produce the potential for more favorable outcomes. At first this may be using your knowledge of one particular ingredient to enhance a situation, address a problem, or strengthen the long-term relationship you are in the process of developing. Applying ahimsa to the process of negotiation, being mindful of gender norms within the team with which you are working, or modifying the time of meetings to suit family priorities are all small ways to partake of the ingredients to experiment with how they work, and the qualities they offer to the overall functionality of your team and project.

Mix and Cook: As you become more aware of how each ingredient functions, in which contexts, and what they may add, the next level is to work with multiple ingredients to exponentially increase the efficiency and productivity of the team or partnership with which you are engaged. Your leadership style may take on a balance of just the right percentage of fostering self-emergent responsibility and delegation from within the group, but also acknowledges and works within the expectations of hierarchy at the right moments. Another experiment may be outlining a project according to the steps of a pilgrimage, but adding in to this base some of the components of karma yoga—being impartial to failure and success and looking out for the greatest good. With experience, you will begin to have an innate sense of which ingredients are needed and how to mix them in the right proportion to produce the desired results. Some may need time to simmer, while others need a more quick-flash approach to create the best outcome.

Digest: There are many great things about working with cultural ingredients, and gaining versatility in them. One of the benefits is to reap the rewards of creating strong working relationships with your Indian colleagues. As you build your cultural knowledge over time, you will be able to adapt to more subtle tastes and preferences, reflecting on which mixes work the best for you and your colleagues, as well as what does not. Even as cultural facility becomes second nature, it is important to remember that culture is in a constant state of flux. Your working knowledge of the ingredients needs to be revisited and revised at intervals.

Out of all the ingredients, figuring out your own dharma, or duties, in connection to the roles you fulfill while in India will be invaluable to accomplishing the larger goals you have set out for yourself and the company. What is going to help you to perform at the highest dharmic level is concentrated around becoming a master chef who uses the cultural ingredients with increased skill to provide the best service possible in each context.

Once you have worked with the ingredients—observing, tasting, mixing, cooking, and digesting them—they will become an invaluable part of your toolbox. The aim of this work is to translate these cultural models into tangible, practical means to improve your business interactions in any situation in India. As you gather your files, create presentations, run numbers, become acquainted with background and plans, and work with future projections, don't forget to pack your newfound cultural knowledge in your bag as well. It just may be the most invaluable item that you will never want to leave behind again. Even though you may find yourself increasingly traveling to more countries for business, at least for India, you will be far ahead of the rest as a truly culture-savvy road warrior! Good luck, and may your next trip be more successful than ever!

Appendix

Facts About India: Menu Options

A large majority of businesses and commercial activities in India are clustered in and around four super metro areas, namely Delhi, Mumbai, Chennai, and Kolkata, and big cities such as Bangalore, Hyderabad, Pune, and a few others. The primary reason for such concentration is that the British developed the three port cities of Kolkata, Mumbai, and Chennai as presidency towns, which over time emerged as major educational centers and trading hubs. The first three Indian universities were established in 1857 in these cities. Kolkata was the capital of British India until 1912 when they moved it to New Delhi. Delhi is not a coastal town and does not have access to a seaport, the primary requirement for movement of goods and cargo. However, after becoming the capital city, Delhi gradually developed as the fourth contemporary metropolis of India. Delhi University was established in 1916 and with time the city started emerging as a prominent center for education and business. Lack of infrastructure and other support systems outside these cities also led to clustering and overcrowding of industries in and around these cities.

When the IT sector started emerging in the 1980s as a major vehicle of India's technical and business prowess, Infosys's decision to locate its headquarters in Bangalore put it on the world map. This led to a strategic shift in thinking that helped Bangalore, Hyderabad, and Pune emerge as the new business destinations for IT and other knowledge-based industries. These cities are prominent educational hubs and have hundreds of technical and management institutions located in and around them that churn out engineers and managers by the thousands each year, ensuring a steady supply to meet the increasing demands for these industries. They are also less expensive cities and provide a better quality of life at affordable costs. It's a win-win scenario for both parties. The industry gets bright technical and management graduates aplenty at lower cost and the youth brigade finds vocations that are novel, exciting, and challenging and gives them a decent lifestyle away from the hassles of the metro cities. The nature of the IT industry also helped. Since IT was an entirely new industry with little or no legacy, it did not require regular interaction with government bureaucracy and officials unlike other businesses. As the clientele is largely made of global and multinational corporations from the United States and Europe, the role of government and local agencies is primarily limited to providing a broad legal framework and guidelines for the industry that brings in precious foreign exchange into the country by the millions.

Northern Region

Mumbai

In the northern region, Mumbai, Delhi, and Kolkata are the major centers for business. Even IT and other knowledge-based industries have also been developing in these main cities and around their suburbs such as Gurgaon and NOIDA (New Okhla Industrial Development Authority) in Delhi and Salt Lake City in Kolkata. Only Pune can be considered a new star kid on the block since it is a good 100 miles from Mumbai, but it owes its ascendancy primarily to its relative proximity to this city.

Mumbai is the largest Indian city and is the main hub of banking and financial services in the country besides being the capital of the Indian state of Maharashtra. Traditionally known for its financial services, stock market, textile mills, pharmaceutical companies, and chemical industries the city is home to the Bombay Stock Exchange, National Stock Exchange, major domestic and international banks, investment firms, commercial corporations, and the largest sector of the Indian film industry. Situated on the western coast by the Arabian Sea the greater Mumbai metropolitan area has a population of about 20 million. Mumbai has a tropical climate and weather is moderately warm throughout the year. The city has a seaport, a large international and domestic airport, and a good local bus and suburban train network. India's first railway line was built between Mumbai and Thane in 1853. The Mumbai airport is currently undergoing expansion and modernization and a mass rapid transit system, Mumbai Metro, is being constructed in the city.

Starting out as clusters of fishing communities, Mumbai went through several phases of ownership from Indian kingdoms to that of the Portuguese, who eventually gave it away to the British King Charles II as part of a dowry for marrying their princess Catherine. Since independence in 1947, Mumbai has emerged as a cultural melting pot attracting migrants from all over India drawn by the lure of business opportunities, jobs, education, and films. This put tremendous pressure on land, infrastructure, and civil amenities in the city and led to the mushrooming of slums, widespread poverty, and crimes. Although there is Marathi-Gujarati dominance in the city, all linguistic and ethnic groups of the country are well represented in this megapolis.

Mumbai has a very cosmopolitan culture with a strongly secular and liberal outlook. It is an amalgam made of many religions, customs, and traditions that is reflected in its festivals, music, cuisine, and films. Marathi, Gujarati, Hindi, and English are the main languages spoken in the city. English is the preferred language for business while Hindi is the main medium for Indian films; hundreds of titles are churned out from the city studios and production houses a year. Konkan seafood, Goan delicacies, and some local Marathi fare are popular food choices.

Pune

Historically Pune has been known for its excellent educational institutions, engineering companies, military establishments, and spiritual centers. Earlier, the presence of hundreds of educational institutions in and around the city and abundant availability of technical graduates prompted leading Indian business houses to locate their manufacturing units near the city. Since liberalization of the Indian economy in 1991, the attractiveness of Pune has soared on the strengths of its proximity to Mumbai, lower costs, improving infrastructure, and a higher quality of living index. Pune is home to about five million people and is well connected by air and train to metros and other major Indian cities. Pune is only 100 miles from Mumbai and is connected by an express highway. A local suburban rail network is being planned for the city. Several Indian and global IT services companies have set up their operations in the city to reduce their costs while avoiding the hassles and problems of Mumbai. Its tropical climate and moderate weather are added bonuses.

Although Pune is predominantly Marathi and Hinduism is the main religion, its culture is very tolerant, accommodating, and cosmopolitan. Like other big Indian cities, Pune has many temples, mosques, churches, and religious centers for everyone. Osho's world headquarters is located in a city neighborhood that attracts followers from all over the world and lends a global touch to the local culture. A wide variety of food choices from international cuisine to fast food and local Marathi delicacies are readily available in the city.

Pune played a significant role in India's freedom struggle as leaders from the region, such as G. K. Gokhale and B. G. Tilak, led from the front. Tilak is also credited with popularizing the Ganesh festival as a symbol of national unity in the late 19th century and as a mark of defiance against British rule. Since then, the Ganesh festival has acquired immense popularity and towers over other Hindus festivals as a cultural manifestation of Marathi pride.

Delhi

The Delhi metropolitan area known as the National capital region (NCR) includes the capital city New Delhi, old Delhi, surrounding suburbs of NOIDA, Gurgaon, Ghaziabad, and Faridabad with a combined population of about 18 million. Delhi is the second largest Indian city after Mumbai and has a large international and domestic airport. Northern Railway headquarters is located in the city. A world-class rapid transit system, Delhi Metro, inaugurated in 2003 has improved local transport tremendously. It is likely to complete its Phase II covering nearly 100 miles before October 2010 when Delhi will host the Commonwealth Games. The city is feverishly building and revamping its existing infrastructure for the big event. Most of the major outsourcing firms have a presence here servicing their international clients. This has led to tremendous growth and expansion of the satellite townships of Gurgaon and NOIDA.

Delhi has a subtropic climate characterized by hot summers and cold winters. The city has a unique blend of Mughal and Hindu culture reflected in its buildings, festivals, food, music, and literature. Delhi served as the capital city to many Muslim dynasties in the past. When the British made it their capital in 1912 it brought a wide array of people from many ethnic backgrounds and religions to serve in the British administration. India's partition in 1947 brought a deluge of refugees, primarily Hindus and Sikhs, from the previously undivided Punjab province, adding a Punjabi flavor to the local culture. Delhi is home to some of the best known religious centers for Hindus, Muslims, Sikhs, Baha'i, and other faiths. Hindi and Punjabi are the main spoken languages along with English, which is the primary language for business. Historically, Delhi's major employer has been the federal government and its many allied organizations, but in recent times Delhi and its suburbs have carved a niche for service industries that include IT, BPO, telecommunication, hospitality, retail, media, and other sectors. Delhi is also the most important hub in India's famed tourism triangle of Delhi-Agra-Jaipur.

Delhi hosts an assortment of food choices in its hundreds of eateries. However, the pride of the place is reserved for Mughalai and Punjabi nonvegetarian entrées along with ethnic specialties from nearby regions.

Gurgaon (Haryana State) cut its teeth as an emerging industrial and business hub when the Indian government chose to set up a Suzuki-Maruti automobile manufacturing plant there in the early 1980s. This was closely followed by a Hero-Honda motorcycle plant and other related automotive industries in the area in the mid-1980s. Indian economy unshackled itself from self-imposed restrictions and regulations in 1991 and opened its doors for business and investment. The local state government anticipated a big opportunity in the new business environment. It revamped its industrial and tax policy, developed real estate, housing, and other infrastructure with private companies in order to attract business and investments. Today Gurgaon is a major outsourcing and off-shore destination for global and Indian corporations. Its other important industries include automobile, real estate, and retail.

Gurgaon's proximity to Delhi was a major attraction. Executives could continue to live in Delhi even after locating their business to the new satellite town, which was less than 20 miles from the city and only 6 miles from the international airport. An eight-lane expressway currently connects Delhi with Gurgaon; by the end of 2010, Delhi metro will also arrive there, enhancing its attractiveness as a business destination since the commute will be less than an hour without any hassles of traffic.

NOIDA (Uttar Pradesh State) is the other main business suburb of the National Capital Region, which is only 10 miles southeast of Delhi and is now conveniently connected by Delhi Metro. Envisioned as an industrial hub and special economic zone in the 1970s, today NOIDA is home to hundreds of manufacturing, electronics, media, telecom, software, IT, and BPO companies. Its sprawling township also houses several reputed schools, colleges, hospitals, and technical institutions of excellence serving the needs of its residents and industries.

Kolkata

Kolkata was the capital of British India until 1911 and India's largest city until the 1980s. Situated on the banks of the Hooghly River, and with a population of over 15 million, Kolkata is the most important hub of education, industry, and commerce in eastern India in addition to being the capital of West Bengal. Its emergence as an industrial powerhouse on the strengths of its textile, jute, and automobile industries led to its enormous growth and prominence. British patronage and investments in infrastructure helped it to become a great center for education, business, art, and philosophy. Kolkata is served by a seaport and has a large international and domestic airport connecting it to major cities of India and those of South East Asia. The first underground suburban rail network in India, Kolkata Metro, was launched in the city in the mid-1980s. The city is the seat of the Kolkata Stock exchange and houses the headquarters of several public sector banks, government undertakings, and private sector companies.

A socialist government ruling the state since 1977 and the presence of a very active trade union in the city have been major hindrances for Kolkata in attracting new business and capital. Many business houses that were earlier located in the city have since moved to other places. The current state government has been trying to inculcate a business-friendly culture for the last few years and several Indian and foreign corporations in IT and other sectors have been working from Salt Lake City Software Technology Park, but the general atmosphere remains uncertain for growth. Recent disputes involving the state government and local farmers over land acquisition for Tata Nano and other SEZ (special economic zone) projects have done severe damage to the prospects of attracting new business and capital.

Kolkata has a tropical climate with hot and humid summers followed by short and mild winters. Kolkata is the birthplace of Nobel laureate Rabindranath Tagore and is known as the "Cultural capital of India" due to its long association with literature, art, philosophers, and firebrand nationalists. Kolkata's profoundly Hindu-Bengali culture is reflected in its worship of Devi, the Great Goddess, fish dishes, music (Rabindra *Sangeet*, Baul), theater (*jatra*), cinema, and dance (*bihu*, *chhau*). However, the city has a metropolitan outlook and strong secular credentials. Unlike other cities and the rest of India where cricket is worshipped like a religion, soccer is immensely popular in Kolkata and has a huge fan following.

Southern Region

In the southern region, the most important centers for business and commerce are the erstwhile presidency town of Madras renamed as Chennai and the two shining stars of the IT industry, namely Bangalore and Hyderabad. Bangalore is often referred to as the Silicon Valley of India.

Bangalore

Historically Bangalore was known as a retirees' haven due to its moderate climate and leafy, quiet suburbs with lots of sunshine. Bangalore is the largest city in the southern region of India and is the capital of Karnataka state. It is home to over eight million people and is also the seat of the vernacular Kannada film industry. It is well connected with the rest of India by air and railways. A new international airport was built in 2008 to meet the demands of ever increasing air traffic. A rapid transit system is being built in the city to improve intra-city and suburban transport requirements. Kannada, Tamil, Telugu, Hindi, and English are the main spoken languages. Hindi films have immense popularity in the city.

Although Bangalore is home to several private corporations, public sector undertakings, space and scientific establishments, it was Infosys that transformed its image and laid its foundation as India's Silicon Valley. Texas Instruments was the first global corporation to set up its base in the city in the mid-1980s. Soon after, many other domestic and international IT companies followed suit. Today, Bangalore boasts the presence of a galaxy of Fortune 500 companies, primarily in technology and IT services sectors. What Mumbai is for banking and financial services Bangalore is for IT and technology services industries.

Bangalore has a very moderate tropical climate and the weather is quite pleasant throughout the year. Bangalore's culture is very cosmopolitan with a global outlook. Though people of Kannada and Tamil descent dominate the population, the city is increasingly becoming a microcosm of India as companies based in the city and its surrounding suburbs attract migrants from all over the country and even abroad. The presence of a large number of reputed technical, scientific, and management institutions in and around the city, which boast of a pan-Indian kaleidoscope, has also added to its changing demographic profile. An amazing array of food choices is available in the city due to its rapid modernization and the presence of several hospitality and food chains. The city has a predominantly Hindu population that is reflected in its culture, festivals, and other traditions. However, in the 18th century the city was part of the Mysore kingdom ruled by the great nationalists Hyder Ali and Tipu Sultan, who eventually lost power to the British but left behind a notable Muslim culture that continues to thrive.

Hyderabad

Hyderabad is the other shining star of India's IT industry. Home to over 6.5 million people it is the largest city and capital of Andhra Pradesh. Telugu, Urdu, Hindi, and English are the main spoken languages. The city is also home to the popular Telugu film industry. A new international airport was inaugurated in 2008 to keep up with the increasing demands of air traffic.

Historically Hyderabad has been famous for its association with the Nizam, his palaces and jewels. The Nizams ruled the Hyderabad region until Indian independence in 1947 and can trace their lineage to Nizam-ul-Mulk, the governor of Deccan under the Mughals in the early 1720s, who revolted, carved out an independent state, and declared himself as the sovereign ruler. However, the credit for putting Hyderabad on the world map goes to Chandra Babu Naidu who took over as the chief minister of the state in the mid-1990s. He helped usher in an IT revolution in the city by establishing a dedicated suburb, HITEC City, and by offering ready infrastructure and attractive tax and other incentives to the best and most reputed IT companies in the world for setting up their operations in the city. Today, Hyderabad prides itself as the home to several global and Indian corporations. Pharmaceuticals and biotechnology are other prominent industries. Hundreds of technical, management, scientific, space, and defense institutions and establishments have also played a significant role in the emergence of Hyderabad as a modern and forward looking global city.

The climate of Hyderabad is tropical with hot summers and a mild winter. The culture of Hyderabad is a unique blend of several cultures and traditions and reflects a fusion of many Hindu and Persian elements. The local dialect is a unique blend of Urdu, Hindi, and Telugu languages. Dress choices display an array of Persian, Hindu, and Western tastes. Charminar, Golkonda fort, Balaji temple, and St. Joseph's church are some of the famous landmarks found here. Hyderabad is home to Raja and Radha Reddy, the renowned exponents of Kuchipudi dance, a classical Indian dance form that originated in the state of Andhra Pradesh. Hyderabad is also famous for its cuisine, which reflects the strong influence of Hindu, Mughal, and Persian food traditions. Hyderabadi biryani, an entrée made of rice and mutton or chicken with distinctive spices, is a specialty and proud tradition in the city.

Chennai

Chennai is the changed name of the erstwhile British presidency town of Madras. Situated on the eastern coast of the Bay of Bengal, Chennai is the capital of the state of Tamil Nadu and home to about 7.5 million people. Chennai has a seaport, and a large international and domestic airport that connects it to major cities in India and South East Asia. While Chennai has an operational suburban rail network, a mass rapid transit system is currently under construction. Tamil and English are the main spoken languages. Chennai is also home to the second largest film industry after Mumbai.

Chennai has built a strong industrial and business culture since the British days. Traditionally a prominent hub of automobile and chemical industries it has emerged as a major center for automobile and electronics manufacturing in recent years. Many Indian and global corporations have set up their manufacturing units in and around the city. Chennai also houses many banks and financial services companies and has a thriving biotechnology and IT services sector. Chennai is surrounded by eminent institutions of technology, engineering, research, health care, and management.

Chennai has a tropical climate with hot and humid summers and a relatively short and mild winter. Known as the center of the Indian classical dance form of Bharatanatyam and Carnatic music, Chennai is the high priestess of many rich cultural traditions and home to many famous temples and religious festivals. Chennai has been traditionally very conservative, built on old orthodox Hindu traditions. However, the onslaught of modernity, increasing industrialization, and globalization is transforming Chennai into a much more cosmopolitan city. It is emerging as a unique blend where the new coexists beautifully with the old and showcases India's amazing diversity. Although many city restaurants serve a nonvegetarian and continental menu, Chennai food is predominantly vegetarian, especially *sambhar*, or lentil based stews, and *rasam*, a tamarind-based broth, both served over rice. Even breakfast food and snacks are primarily made of rice and lentils, including *idli* and *dosai*, and are enjoyed with a variety of coconut, mint, and tomato chutneys. Local Tamil festivals, such as Pongal, are celebrated along with Navaratri, Diwali, Eid, and Christmas.

Notes

Chapter 1

1. Gavin Flood, *An Introduction to Hinduism* (Cambridge: Cambridge University Press, 1996), 21. The dates of the Indus Valley Civilization are debated, and so the dates given may be different depending on the source. We have chosen to cite Flood's scholarly timeline.

2. As the census Web site for India is currently unavailable, please see the Pew Forum for Religion and Public Life, "Religious Demographic Profile: India," based on the 2001 census, http://pewforum.org/world-affairs/countries/?CountryID=94 (accessed March 15, 2010).

3. Thomas Friedman, *The World Is Flat: A Brief History of the Twenty-First Century*, 2nd ed., rev. (New York: Farrar, Straus, and Giroux, 2007), 60–77.

4. India Brand Equity Foundation, "Indian Economy Review," December 2009, http://www.ibef.org/economy/economyoverview.aspx (accessed March 5, 2010).

5. India Brand Equity Foundation, "Economic Survey 2009–10," February 2010, http://www.ibef.org/economy/economicsurvey2010.aspx (accessed March 5, 2010).

6. Erick Schonfeld, "Dell Bulks Up on IT Consulting with $3.9 Billion Acquisition of Perot Systems," *TechCrunch*, September 21, 2009, http://techcrunch.com/2009/09/21/dell-bulks-up-on-it-consulting-with-3-9-billion-acquisition-of-perot-systems/ (accessed March 5, 2010).

7. "Indian Maritime Industry is Poised for a Sea Change," *The Financial Express*, October 27, 2008, http://www.financialexpress.com/printer/news/378480/ (accessed March 5, 2010).

8. Tarun Shukla and K. Raghu, "GVK buys 12% in Bangalore Airport, Wants Majority Stake," Livemint.com, November 6, 2009, http://www.livemint.com/2009/11/06000130/GVK-buys-12-in-Bangalore-airp.html (accessed March 24, 2010).

9. Ratna Bhushan and Kala Vijayaraghavan, "Cadbury Buyout Gives Kraft Foods Access to India," *The Economic Times*, January 20, 2010, http://

168 Notes

economictimes.indiatimes.com/news/news-by-industry/cons-products/food/Cadbury-buyout-gives-Kraft-Foods-access-to-India/articleshow/5478284.cms (accessed March 5, 2010).

10. "Govt Okays Bill, Foreign Varsities in India Soon," *Hindustan Times*, March 16, 2010, http://www.hindustantimes.com/News-Feed/india/Government-okays-bill-foreign-varsities-in-India-soon/Article1-519512.aspx (accessed March 24, 2010).

11. Harvard Business School Release, "Harvard Business School Extends Global Presence with India Research Center in Mumbai," November 2, 2005, http://www.hbs.edu/news/releases/india.html (accessed March 4, 2010).

12. Las Vegas Convention and Visitors Authority, Research Department, 2008, "Vegas FAQs," http://www.lvcva.com/getfile/2008%20Vegas%20FAQs.pdf?fileID=106 (accessed November 23, 2009).

13. Himanshu, "Counting the Poor: A Poverty of Statistics," September 9, 2008, Livemint.com, *Wall Street Journal*, http://www.livemint.com/articles/2008/09/09232719/Counting-the-poor-a-poverty-o.html (accessed March 25, 2010); and World Bank Group, "India at a Glance," Statistics for 2008, published December 9, 2009.

Chapter 3

1. The Smithsonian Institute has an ongoing exhibit on puja and a useful Web site on the topic: http://www.asia.si.edu/pujaonline/puja/background.html.

2. One of the earliest documented examples of this concept is found in the *Taittiriya Upanisad* (I.11.1–6). See Patrick Olivelle, trans., *Upanisads* (New York: Oxford University Press, 1996).

3. Diana Eck, *Darsan: Seeing the Divine Image in India* (New York: Columbia University Press, 1998), 1.

Chapter 4

1. The connection between a person's role and the dharma that corresponds to that role is so important that even when the role contains some ethical issues the focus keeps getting put back on how well the duties are fulfilled. An unusual example of this is analyzed by A. Passi, who writes of the dharma of a thief, as narrated in an ancient text on duty, the *Dharmacauryarasayana*. See A. Passi, "Perverted Dharma Ethics of Thievery in the *Dharmacauryarasayana*," *Journal of Indian Philosophy* 33, no. 4 (August 2005): 513–28. I am indebted to Kirti Vaswani for pointing out this nuance to dharma.

2. Zeus Air Services Pvt. Ltd., "Corporate Philosophy," http://www.zeuslogistics.com/cp.htm (accessed November 24, 2009).

3. Gurucharan Das, "The Dharma of Capitalism: Timely Lessons from Indian Philosophy," *The Wall Street Journal*, April 22, 2009, http://online.wsj.com/article/SB124034244071240085.html (accessed March 5, 2010).

4. Daniel Burke, "Dow Jones Unveils 'Dharma Index'," *Religion News Service* (January 16, 2008), http://pewforum.org/news/rss.php?NewsID=14776 (accessed March 18, 2009).

5. Lewis Lazare, "Crisis Triggered Brilliant PR Response," *Chicago Sun-Times*, News Special Edition (September 29, 2002), 19.

Chapter 5

1. *Rig Veda* 10.90 (The Hymn of Man). See *The Rig Veda, an Anthology of One Hundred Eight Hymns*, trans. Wendy Doniger (New York: Penguin Classics, 1982), 231.

2. Gerald Larson, *India's Agony Over Religion* (New York: State University of New York Press, 1995), 261–66.

3. Other religious communities, in particular Christians and Muslims in India, have created their own internal caste systems that are similar to the Hindu model discussed in this chapter.

4. According to Dalit International Foundation, point number 7, there are no dalits who currently occupy the position of CEO in the top 100 industrialists category. http://www.dalitinternational.org/About%20the%20Crusader/Vital%20Statistics%20About%20Dalits%20.html (accessed November 22, 2009).

5. Geert Hofstede, "Cultural Dimensions," http://www.geert-hofstede.com. Societies with a high power ranking are more likely to have systems in place that do not allow significant upward mobility of its citizens, while a low power ranking indicates a de-emphasis of differences between a citizen's power and wealth and opportunities for growth and equality, regardless of position.

Chapter 6

1. Victor Turner, *The Ritual Process: Structure and Anti-Structure* (New York: Gruyter, 1969), 96.

Chapter 7

1. C. K. Prahalad and M. S. Krishnan, *The New Age of Innovation* (New York: McGraw Hill, 2008), 69–70.

2. Nrupesh Mastakar and B. Bowonder, "Transformation of an Entrepreneurial Firm to a Global Service Provider: The Case Study of Infosys," *International Journal of Technology Management* 32, nos. 1/2 (2005): 34–56.

3. Shishir Bhate, "How Infosys Grooms its Future Leaders," *Rediff India Abroad*, August 3, 2006, www.rediff.com/money/2006/aug/03mspec.htm (accessed February 2, 2010).

Chapter 8

1. Two translations of the *Bhagavad Gita* (Song of the Lord) available in English that we recommend for further reading are translated by Barbara Stoler Miller (New York: Bantam, 1986) and Laurie L. Patton (New York: Penguin, 2008).

2. C. K. Prahalad, *The Fortune At the Bottom of the Pyramid* (Philadelphia, PA: Wharton School Publishing, 2006), 131–35.

Chapter 9

1. In the *Vedas*, other figures are connected to ideas of wealth, including Kubera.

2. Vasudha Narayanan, a scholar of Asian Religions, is among the first to speak of Hindu gods "gaining visas" to live in temples outside of India according to their placement on a scale of benevolence and prosperity on the one hand, and fierce, violent protectors, such as Kali, on the other.

3. The Indian Constitution does not recognize property rights as a fundamental right. It originally provided for the right to property under Articles 19 and 31. Article 19 guaranteed Indian citizens the right to acquire, hold, and dispose of property while Article 31 provided that "no person shall be deprived of his property save by authority of law." But in 1978, the 44th amendment eliminated the right to "acquire, hold and dispose of property" as a fundamental right. However, in another part of the Constitution, Article 300 (A) was inserted to affirm that, "no person shall be deprived of his property save by authority of law." The result is that the right to property is now substituted as a statutory right. The amendment expanded the power of the state to appropriate property for "social welfare purposes."

4. Kaushik Basu, "Phenomenal Rise of India's Savings," *BBC News*, April 17, 2007, http://news.bbc.co.uk/2/hi/south_asia/6544111.stm (accessed November 10, 2009).

5. Dhruv Rathi and Ashish Gupta, "Unleashing Equity Cult: Dhirubhai Ambani Changed the Plot for Corporate India and Scripted an Equity Growth Story That Will Never End," *Outlook Business Magazine*, August 20, 2007, http://business.outlookindia.com/article.aspx?100110 (accessed November 15, 2009).

6. "Remittance: India Again Tops the World," *Rediff Business,* July 27, 2009, http://business.rediff.com/slide-show/2009/jul/27/slide-show-1-remittance-india-again-tops-the-world.htm (accessed November 15, 2009).

7. Tarun Khanna, *Billions of Entrepreneurs: How China and India Are Reshaping Their Futures and Yours* (Cambridge, MA: Harvard Business School Press, 2007).

8. Dean Nelson, "Where Are India's Great Philanthropists?" *Telegraph.co.uk,* July 28, 2009, http://blogs.telegraph.co.uk/news/deannelson/100004813/where-are-indias-great-philanthropists/ (accessed October 5, 2009).

9. Priya Viswanath and Noshir Dadrawala, *Philanthropy and Equity: The Case of India* (Cambridge, MA: Global Equity Initiative, Harvard University, 2004), 8, 17–20.

10. Fareed Zakaria, *The Post-American World* (New York: W.W. Norton & Company, 2008), 73–77, 81–86.

11. Charles R. Morris, *The Tycoons: How Andrew Carnegie, John D. Rockefeller, Jay Gould, and J. P. Morgan Invented the American Supereconomy* (New York: Henry Holt and Company, 2005), 13–20.

12. Max Weber, *The Protestant Ethic and the Spirit of Capitalism*, trans. Peter Baehr and Gordon C. Wells (New York: Penguin, 2002).

13. James Hudnut-Beumler, *In Pursuit of the Almighty's Dollar: A History of Money and American Protestantism* (Chapel Hill: University of North Carolina Press, 2007), 47–75.

Chapter 11

1. King Ashoka (third century B.C.E.) united India under Buddhist principles, as evidenced by edicts carved into stone pillars found throughout his empire. He sent his son and daughter, who were ordained into the Buddhist community, to Sri Lanka to create a political alliance that utilized Buddhist principles, rather than conquest. As Buddhism spread, many other countries had similar stories, including the introduction of Buddhism into Japan in the sixth century C.E. by way of gifts from Korea that included Buddhist scriptures and monks. Examples of travel accounts to India include those by Buddhist monks, such as: Fa-Hien, *Record of Buddhistic Kingdoms*, trans. James Legge (Teddington, England: Echo Library, 2006) and Huen-Tsang, *Buddhist Records of the Western World: Translated from the Chinese by Hiuen Tsiang*, trans. Samuel Beal Si-Yu-Ki (New Delhi: Motilal Banarsidass, 2005). Tales of Greek and Roman encounters with India can be found in the work of Grant Parker, *The Making of Roman India* (Cambridge: Cambridge University Press, 2008).

2. David Hardiman, *Gandhi in His Time and Ours: The Global Legacy of His Ideas* (New York: Columbia University Press, 2003), 58–59.

3. Glyn Richards, *The Philosophy of Gandhi: A Study of His Basic Ideas* (Richmond, UK: Curzon Press, 1991), 48–49.

4. M. K. Gandhi, *Non-Violence in Peace & War*, 2 vols. (Ahmedabad: Navajivan Publishing House, 1942), 1:123.

5. Gandhi writes, "In the dictionary of satyagraha there is no enemy" (*Non-Violence in Peace & War*, 1:229); and Mark Juergensmeyer, *Gandhi's Way: A Handbook of Conflict Resolution* (Berkeley: University of California Press, 1984), 27–37, 59–61.

6. In Gandhi's words, "But in the empire of non-violence every true thought counts, every true voice has its full value" (*Non-Violence in Peace & War*, 1:419).

7. Juergensmeyer quotes Gandhi: "As the means, so the end" (*Gandhi's Way*, 40).
8. Gandhi writes, "One has to speak out and stand up for one's convictions" (*Non-Violence in Peace & War*, 2:55).
9. Juergensmeyer, *Gandhi's Way*, 3–11.
10. Gandhi writes, "A non-violent revolution is not a programme [*sic*] of seizure of power. It is a programme of transformation of relationships, ending in a peaceful transfer of power" (*Non-Violence in Peace & War*, 2:10).
11. "Infosys and Growing Revenue from Happy Customers," post by tradinghelpdesk (July 11, 2009), http://tradinghelpdesk.wordpress.com/2009/07/11/infosys-and-growing-revenue-from-happy-customers/ (accessed September 4, 2009).
12. Roger Fisher and William Ury, *Getting to Yes: Negotiating Agreement Without Giving In* (New York: Penguin Books, 1981).
13. Richards, *The Philosophy of Gandhi*, 54–55.
14. Juergensmeyer, *Gandhi's Way*, 33–37.

Chapter 13

1. Alecca, e-mail message with the author, October 9, 2009.
2. Savitri (not her real name), e-mail message with the author, July 23, 2009.
3. Ekta Kapoor, "The Storyteller," interview with N. Amarnath and D. Ghosh, *The Voyage to Excellence: The Ascent of 21 Women Leaders of India, Inc.* (Delhi: Pustak Mahal, 2005), 39.
4. Lalita D. Gupte, "Sporting the Leader's Badge," in *The Voyage to Excellence* (see note 3), 76.
5. Naina Lal Kidwai, "The Master Strategist," in *The Voyage to Excellence* (see note 3), 93.
6. Sulajja Firodia Motwani, "Riding to the Summit," in *The Voyage to Excellence* (see note 3), 235.
7. Tarjani Vakil, "The Pacesetter," in *The Voyage to Excellence* (see note 3), 242–43.
8. Kidwai, "The Master Strategist," 92.
9. A. Pandey, "Sexual Harassment at the Workplace: Implement the Guidelines," *Newsblaze*, January 20, 2009, http://newsblaze.com/story/20090120134229tsop.nb/topstory.html (accessed March 20, 2010); and Neeta Raymond, "Sexual Harassment at Work," *India Together* (Republished online from *Combat Today*, vol. 2:3, August–September 2003, http://www.indiatogether.org/combatlaw/vol2/issue3/harass.htm (accessed March 20, 2010).
10. Savitri, e-mail message with author, July 23, 2009.
11. Alecca, e-mail message with author, October 9, 2009.
12. Gabriela, e-mail message with author, October 27, 2009.
13. Gabriela, e-mail message with author, October 27, 2009.

14. Gabriela, e-mail message with author, October 27, 2009.
15. Savitri, e-mail message with author, July 23, 2009.
16. Ravina Raj Kohli, "Maiden of the Media," in *The Voyage to Excellence* (see note 3), 154.
17. Ritu Kumar, "Refashioning Indian Glamour," in *The Voyage to Excellence* (see note 3), 179.
18. Kumar, "Refashioning Indian Glamour," 179.
19. Preetha Reddy, "Touching Lives," in *The Voyage to Excellence* (see note 3), 107.
20. Shahnaz Hussain, "The Herbal Crusader," in *The Voyage to Excellence* (see note 3), 202.
21. Reddy, "Touching Lives," 106.
22. Savitri, e-mail message with the author, July 23, 2009.
23. Swasti Mitter, Grace Fernandez, and Shaiby Varghese, "On the Threshold of Informalization: Women Call Centre Workers in India," in *Chains of Fortune: Linking Women Producers and Workers with Global Markets*, ed. Marilyn Carr (United Kingdom: Commonwealth Secretariat, 2004). From Box 1, 169.
24. Chanda Kocchar, "Better than the Best," in *The Voyage to Excellence* (see note 3), 32.
25. Rajshree Pathy, "The Candy-maker," in *The Voyage to Excellence* (see note 3), 131.
26. Gupte, "Sporting the Leader's Badge," 78.
27. Motwani, "Riding to the Summit," 235.
28. Stacy Blake-Beard, "Mentoring as a Bridge to Cultural Understanding," unpublished article, 2009.

Chapter 14

1. Ryszard Kapuscinski, *Travels with Herodotus*, trans. Klara Glowczewska (New York: Alfred A. Knopf, 2007), 39.
2. Rama Bijapurkar, *Winning in the Indian Market: Understanding the Transformation of Consumer India* (New York: John Wiley & Sons, 2007), 139.
3. Saritha Rai, "Taste of India in U.S. Wrappers," *New York Times*, April 29, 2003, http://www.nytimes.com/2003/04/29/business/tastes-of-india-in-us-wrappers.html (accessed November 30, 2009).
4. Pawan Chabra, "Some Bumps Ahead But Not a Dead End," *The Sunday Indian*, October 11, 2009.
5. Nokia, "Nokia India," http://www.nokia.co.in/about-nokia/company (accessed November 28, 2009).
6. Moinak Mitra and Bhanu Pande, "How Nokia Became India's Largest MNC," *The Economic Times*, June 5, 2009, http://economictimes.indiatimes.com/features/corporate-dossier/How-Nokia-became-Indias-largest-MNC/articleshow/4619036.cms (accessed March 25, 2010).

Bibliography

Amarnath, Nischinta, and Debashish Ghosh. *The Voyage to Excellence: The Ascent of 21 Women Leaders of India, Inc.* Delhi: Pustak Mahal, 2005.

Bijapurkar, Rama. *Winning in the Indian Market: Understanding the Transformation of Consumer India.* New York: John Wiley & Sons, 2007.

Blake-Beard, Stacy. "Mentoring as a Bridge to Cultural Understanding," unpublished article, 2009.

Doniger, Wendy, trans. *The Rig Veda, an Anthology of One Hundred Eight Hymns.* New York: Penguin Classics, 1982.

Eck, Diana. *Darsan: Seeing the Divine Image in India.* New York: Columbia University Press, 1998.

Fisher, Roger, and William Ury. *Getting to Yes: Negotiating Agreement Without Giving In.* New York: Penguin Books, 1981.

Flood, Gavin. *An Introduction to Hinduism.* Cambridge, UK: Cambridge University Press, 1996.

Friedman, Thomas. *The World Is Flat: A Brief History of the Twenty-First Century,* 2nd ed. rev. New York: Farrar, Straus, and Giroux, 2007.

Gandhi, M. K. *Non-Violence in Peace & War,* 2 vols. Ahmedabad: Navajivan Publishing House, 1942.

Hardiman, David. *Gandhi in His Time and Ours: The Global Legacy of His Ideas.* New York: Columbia University Press, 2003.

Hudnut-Beumler, James. *In Pursuit of the Almighty's Dollar: A History of Money and American Protestantism.* Chapel Hill: University of North Carolina Press, 2007.

Juergensmeyer, Mark. *Gandhi's Way: A Handbook of Conflict Resolution.* Berkeley: University of California Press, 1984.

Kapuscinski, Ryszard. *Travels with Herodotus,* trans. Klara Glowczewska. New York: Alfred A. Knopf, 2007.

Khanna, Tarun. *Billions of Entrepreneurs: How China and India Are Reshaping Their Futures and Yours.* Cambridge, MA: Harvard Business School Press, 2007.

Larson, Gerald. *India's Agony Over Religion.* New York: State University of New York Press, 1995.

Lazare, Lewis. "Crisis Triggered Brilliant PR Response." *Chicago Sun-Times*, September 29, 2002, News Special Edition.

Mastakar, Nrupesh, and B. Bowonder. "Transformation of an Entrepreneurial Firm to a Global Service Provider: The Case Study of Infosys." *International Journal of Technology Management* 32, no. 1/2 (2005): 34–56.

Miller, Barbara Stoler, trans. *The Bhagavad-Gita: Krishna's Counsel in Time of War*. New York: Bantam, 1986.

Mitter, Swasti, Grace Fernandez, and Shaiby Varghese. "On the Threshold of Informalization: Women Call Centre Workers in India." In *Chains of Fortune: Linking Women Producers and Workers with Global Markets*, edited by Marilyn Carr, 165–85. United Kingdom: Commonwealth Secretariat, 2004.

Morris, Charles R. *The Tycoons: How Andrew Carnegie, John D. Rockefeller, Jay Gould, and J. P. Morgan Invented the American Supereconomy*. New York: Henry Holt and Company, 2005.

Olivelle, Patrick, trans. *Upanisads*. New York: Oxford University Press, 1996.

Patton, Laurie L., trans. *The Bhagavad Gita*. New York: Penguin, 2008.

Prahalad, C. K. *The Fortune at the Bottom of the Pyramid*. Philadelphia, PA: Wharton School Publishing, 2006.

Prahalad, C. K., and M. S. Krishnan. *The New Age of Innovation*. New York: McGraw Hill, 2008.

Richards, Glyn. *The Philosophy of Gandhi: A Study of his Basic Ideas*. Richmond, UK: Curzon Press, 1991.

Turner, Victor. *The Ritual Process: Structure and Anti-Structure*. New York: Gruyter, 1969.

Viswanath, Priya, and Noshir Dadrawala. "Philanthropy and Equity: The Case of India." Cambridge, MA: Global Equity Initiative, Harvard University, 2004.

Weber, Max. *The Protestant Ethic and the Spirit of Capitalism*, trans. Peter Baehr and Gordon C. Wells. New York: Penguin, 2002.

Zakaria, Fareed. *The Post-American World*. New York: W.W. Norton & Company, 2008.

Index

Acknowledgment: teamwork, 66–68
Adjusting to India: Canon, 151–52; IT companies, 145–46; McDonald's, 146–48; Nokia, 149–51; Suzuki, 148–49
Agni, 98
Agriculture, 14–15
Ahimsa (nonviolence): critique, 117–18; cultural and religious practices, 110–11; nonconfrontational negotiation analogy, 23, 110
Airports, 13
Aravind Eye Hospital, 82
Arjuna, 76

Bangalore, 11, 157, 163–64
Bhagavad Gita, 4, 22, 76
Blake-Beard, Stacy, 141
Body language, 109–10
Bollywood, 8, 15–16
Bombay. *See* Mumbai
Buddhism: ahimsa, 110; Indian religious history, 4; sharing wealth, 92
Business: dress code, 6–7; family run, 5
Business process outsourcing (BPO), 5, 9, 11–12, 37, 145–46; working hours, 123–24, 133

Calcutta. *See* Kolkata
Call centers. *See* Business process outsourcing
Calvin, John, 93
Canon, 151–52

Caste, 19; business hierarchy analogy, 21; illegality of discrimination under Indian Constitution, 47; origin in Veda, 46–47; reservation system, 47–48. *See also* Dalit
Chennai, 14, 157, 165–66
China, 10, 14
Christianity, 5, 92–95; influence on ahimsa, 110–11
Cisco Systems, 11, 146
Clothing, 6–7
Communitas, 59
Conflict: hierarchy and power, 48–50; role conflict, 38–40
Context: business, 20
Contract negotiation. *See* Negotiation
Cultural illiteracy, 145
Cyclical time, 122–24

Dalit, 47–48
Darshan (to see and be seen), 30–31
Das, Gurucharan, 41
Decisions: karma yoga analogy, 76–81
Delhi, 13, 157, 160–62
Dharma (duty), 21, 36–44; Dow Jones Index, 42; failure of, 41
Durga, 138
Duty. *See* Dharma

Eck, Diana, 30
Economy: deregulation, 91, 161; growth, 10; overview, 8–10
Education, 15; women, 132
Eve-teasing. *See* Sexual harassment

Index

Exchange: in hospitality, 30–32
Executives, 49–50

Family: businesses, 6; values, 5, 126
Festivals, 7
Film industry, 15–16
Fire sacrifice: business contract analogy, 22
Fisher, Roger, 116
Food, 6–7; as gifts, 31–33; hospitality, 26–30; McDonald's, 147
Formality: in business culture, 49–50
Four aims of life, 37, 41, 85–86
Friedman, Thomas, 9

Gandhi, Mohandas (Mahatma), 47, 96, 110–11, 115
Ganesh, 37, 127, 160
Gender: bias, 24; roles, 37
Gifts and gifting, 26–33
Globalization, 11
Goals: project process, 62–64
Government: education, 15; health care, 15; illegality of caste discrimination, 47; overview, 3–4
Greetings, 27
Gross domestic product (GDP), 8–9
Growth rate, 8, 10
Guests: role and importance, 27–33

Health care, 15
Hierarchy: caste analogy, 46–54; information access, 51; leadership, 65–70; liaison, 52–53; networking, 51–53; socializing, 49; space and height as markers, 128–29
Highways, 12
Hinduism: ahimsa, 110–11; Indian religious history, 4; risk and action, 76; view of divinities, 27, 30–31; wealth, 85–89, 92–96. *See also* Caste
History: economy, 8–10; overview, 1–4
Hofstede, Geert, 49
Hospitality, 16, 21; hierarchy considerations, 53–54; McDonald's success, 147; meetings, 26; puja (worship) analogy, 26–33; religious context, 26–31; sexual harassment, 137

Hosts, 31–32
Hyderabad, 157, 164–65

ICICI, 65, 134
Indian Stretched Time (IST), 23, 112–13; cultural and religious basis, 123–24; in IT companies, 146
Individual roles, 36–38
Indus Valley Civilization, 1
Informality, 103–4
Information access: hierarchy issues, 51
Information technology (IT), 5, 9–10; Bangalore and Hyderabad, 163–65; success with American companies, 145–46
Infosys, 6, 12, 68, 72–73, 116, 157, 163
Infrastructure, 12–14
Islam: Indian religious history, 4; leadership and teamwork, 66–67; time and space considerations, 122, 125; wealth, 87–88

Jainism: ahimsa, 110; Indian religious history, 4
Jati (occupational group). *See* Caste
Juergensmeyer, Mark, 115, 117

Karma yoga: defined 22; philanthropy, 82; risk and action analogy, 76–81; success, 83–84
Kolkata, 13, 157, 162–63
Krishna, 76

Lakshmi, 37, 85
Languages, 5
Leadership, 22, 65–73; collective leadership, 72–73; teamwork integration, 67–70; women, 133–35, 138–40
Liaison, 53, 98–100
Linear time, 122–24

Madras. *See* Chennai
Mahabharata, 76
Management, 55–64; Suzuki's success, 148
Managers: 49–50
Mandal Commission, 47

Manufacturing, 14
McDonald's, 146–48
Media. *See* Television; Film industry
Meetings: hospitality, 26; Indian Stretched Time, 123
Metallurgy, 14
Middle class, 16–17
Mining, 14
Mission: dharma of, 40–42; Nokia's success, 150
Modernization, 92
Monuments. *See* History
Mumbai: 13, 15, 157–59; film industry in, 8, 15
Music, 7–8
Muslims. *See* Islam

Negotiation: appropriate requests, 101–3; basis of relationships, 104–6, 115–16; contract negotiations, 23, 97; counter-productivity of intimidation, 114–15; fire sacrifice analogy, 97–98; goals, 113–14; hospitality, 115; identifying negotiator, 111–12; intermediation, 98–100; nonconfrontational, 109–10; time and duration, 112–13; verbal contracts, 102–7
Networking, 51–53; in negotiations, 99
New Delhi. *See* Delhi
NOIDA (New Okhla Industrial Development Authority), 158, 160–62
Nokia, 149–51
Nonviolence. *See* Ahimsa
Northern region, 157–63

Outsourcing, 10, 83, 161

Pacing: projects, 59–62
Pakistan, 3
Philanthropy, 82, 91–92
Pilgrimage: project process and management analogy, 22, 55–57
Political parties, 3–4
Ports, 13

Poverty, 17
Power, 13
Power Distance Index (PDI), 49
Privacy, 105
Project process, 55–64; achievement, 62–64; intent, 57; pacing, 59–62; preparation, 58–59
Protestant work ethic, 93
Puja (worship), 21, 26–33, 85
Pune, 157, 159–60

Quick tips: contracts, 106–7; hierarchy, 53–54; hospitality, 32–33; leadership and teamwork, 73; negotiation, 118; project process, 64; pursuit of wealth, 96; risk and action, 84; role expectations, 43–44; summary, 153–55; time and space, 128–29; women in the workplace, 142

Railways, 12–13
Rama, 38–39
Ramayana, 38–39, 103
Relationship: in negotiation, 104–7, 115–16
Religion: informing hospitality, 26–31; leadership and teamwork, 66–67; overview, 4–5; temples and space, 124–28; time, 122–124; views of wealth, 86–95
Reservation system, 47–48
Responsibilities, 36–44
Risk, 22, 75–76
Role: conflict, 38–40; expectations 21, 35–36; individuals, 36–38; information access, 51; women in leadership, 133–35

Sexual harassment, 24, 135–38
Society: business role, 41–44; values, 5–6
Southern region, 157, 163–66
Space, 23, 119–29; organizing principle, 126–28; sacred space, 124–25; temple analogy, 126–27
Stereotypes: white Western women, 136

Stock Market, 90, 158
Suzuki, 14, 148–49

Tata Nano, 116
Teamwork, 22, 65–73; acknowledgment, 66–67; integration with leadership, 70–73
Television, 8, 15–16
Time, 23, 119–29; astrology, 120–21; cyclical time; festivals and holidays, 121–22; linear time, 122–23
Tithing, 94–95
Tourism, 16; medical, 16

Ury, William, 116

Vaastu (spatial design system), 127
Values: overview, 5–6

Vedas: business ethics, 40; caste, 46–47; leadership, 66
Vishnu, 85

Wealth (artha): 22–23, 85–96
Weber, Max, 93
Women: business wear, 7; education, 132; gender dynamics and leadership, 133–34, 138–40; harassment, 135–37; male colleagues, 133; marriage and work, 139–40; traditional escort, 131–33; workplace, 23–24, 131

Y2K, 9, 145

Zakaria, Fareed, 92
Zeus Air Services, 40

About the Authors

Katherine C. Zubko is an assistant professor of Asian religions in the Department of Religious Studies at the University of North Carolina at Asheville. Dr. Zubko has conducted research as a Fulbright scholar in India and has published articles on performance, ritual, and culture.

Raj R. Sahay holds a Marketing MBA from the University of Illinois at Urbana-Champaign. A gold medalist in Indian History and Culture from Patna University, India, Raj has over a decade of composite working experience in the United States and India with reputed global corporations including Accenture and Canon.

JAICO PUBLISHING HOUSE
Elevate Your Life. Transform Your World.

Established in 1946, Jaico Publishing House is the publisher of stellar authors such as Sri Sri Paramahansa Yogananda, Osho, Robin Sharma, Deepak Chopra, Stephen Hawking, Eknath Easwaran, Sarvapalli Radhakrishnan, Nirad Chaudhuri, Khushwant Singh, Mulk Raj Anand, John Maxwell, Ken Blanchard and Brian Tracy. Our list which has crossed a landmark 2000 titles, is amongst the most diverse in the country, with books in religion, spirituality, mind/body/spirit, self-help, business, cookery, humour, career, games, biographies, fiction, and science.

Jaico has expanded its horizons to become a leading publisher of educational and professional books in management and engineering. Our college-level textbooks and reference titles are used by students countrywide. The success of our academic and professional titles is largely due to the efforts of our Educational and Corporate Sales Divisions.

The late Mr. Jaman Shah established Jaico as a book distribution company. Sensing that independence was around the corner, he aptly named his company Jaico ("Jai" means victory in Hindi). In order to tap the significant demand for affordable books in a developing nation, Mr. Shah initiated Jaico's own publications. Jaico was India's first publisher of paperback books in the English language.

In addition to being a publisher and distributor of its own titles, Jaico is a major distributor of books of leading international publishers such as McGraw Hill, Pearson, Cengage Learning, John Wiley and Elsevier Science. With its headquarters in Mumbai, Jaico has other sales offices in Ahmedabad, Bangalore, Bhopal, Chennai, Delhi, Hyderabad and Kolkata. Our sales team of over 40 executives, direct mail order division, and website ensure that our books effectively reach all urban and rural parts of the country.

SINCE 1946